The Cybersecurity Handbook

By

Trevor Shelwick

© Copyright 2024 by Trevor Shelwick- All rights reserved.

The contents of this book may not be reproduced, duplicated, or transmitted without the direct written permission of the author or publisher.

Under no circumstances will the publisher or author be held liable for any damages, recovery, or financial loss due to the information contained in this book. Neither directly nor indirectly.

Legal Notice:

This book is protected by copyright. This book is for personal use only. You may not modify, distribute, sell, use, quote, or paraphrase any part or content of this book without the permission of the author or publisher.

Disclaimer Notice:

Please note that the information contained in this document is for educational and entertainment purposes only. Every effort has been made to present accurate, current, reliable, and complete information. No warranties of any kind are stated or implied. The reader acknowledges that the author is not offering legal, financial, medical, or professional advice. The contents of this book have been taken from various sources. Please consult a licensed professional before attempting any of the techniques described in this book.

By reading this document, the reader agrees that under no circumstances will the author be liable for any direct or indirect loss arising from the use of the information contained in this document, including but not limited to - errors, omissions, or inaccuracies.

Table of contents

HERE ARE YOUR FREE GIFTS! 7

Chapter 1: Introduction to Cybersecurity 8

  1.1 What is Cybersecurity? 8

  1.2 Cybersecurity's Significance in the Modern World 9

  1.3 Common Misconceptions about Cybersecurity 10

  1.4 How Cybersecurity Affects You 11

  1.5 Key Terms and Concepts in Cybersecurity 12

Chapter 2: Understanding Cyber Threats 14

  2.1 Types of Cyber Threats 14

      2.1.1 Viruses and Worms 15

      2.1.2 Trojan Horses 16

      2.1.3 Ransomware 17

      2.1.4 Phishing 18

      2.1.5 Spyware 20

      2.1.6 Adware 21

      2.1.7 Spam 22

      2.1.8 Man-in-the-Middle (MitM) Attacks 24

      2.1.9 DoS and DDoS Attacks 25

      2.1.10 SQL Injection 26

      2.1.11 Zero-Day Exploits 28

      2.1.12 Drive-by Downloads 29

  2.2 Profile of Cyber Attackers 31

  2.3 Case Studies: Notable Cyber Attacks 32

  2.4 Threats to Personal vs. Corporate Security 34

  2.5 The Global Impact of Cyber Threats 35

Chapter 3: Fundamental Cybersecurity Concepts 37

  3.1 The CIA Triad: Confidentiality, Integrity, Availability 37

  3.2 Basics of Cryptography 38

  3.3 Authentication Methods 40

  3.4 Secure Communication Protocols 41

  3.5 The Role of Anonymity and Privacy 42

Chapter 4: Cybersecurity Best Practices 44

  4.1 Creating Strong Passwords 44

  4.2 Regular Updates and Patch Management 45

  4.3 Principles of Least Privilege 46

4.4 Safe Internet Browsing Habits 48

4.5 Physical Security Measures 49

Chapter 5: Secure Your Devices and Networks 50

5.1 Home Network Security Basics 50

5.2 Securing Personal Computers and Laptops 51

5.3 Protecting Mobile Devices: Phones and Tablets 52

5.4 Securing IoT Devices in the Smart Home 53

5.5 Using Public and Private Wi-Fi Safely 54

Chapter 6: The Role of Antivirus and Firewalls 56

6.1 How Antivirus Software Works 56

6.2 Choosing the Right Antivirus 57

6.3 The Importance of Firewalls 58

6.4 Configuring Firewall Settings 59

6.5 Best Practices for Using Antivirus and Firewalls 60

Chapter 7: Cybersecurity at Work 62

7.1 Security Protocols for the Workplace 62

7.2 Handling Sensitive Data 63

7.3 Compliance Requirements: GDPR, HIPAA 64

7.4 Security Training for Employees 65

7.5 Dealing with Security Breaches 66

Chapter 8: Social Engineering and Human Factors 67

8.1 Understanding Social Engineering Attacks 67

8.2 Examples of Social Engineering Attacks 68

8.3 Training Employees to Recognize Social Engineering Attacks ...69

8.4 Building a Security Culture at Work 70

8.5 Personal Vigilance: Protecting Yourself and Others 72

Chapter 9: Introduction to Risk Management 73

9.1 Basics of Cybersecurity Risk Assessment 73

9.2 Tools and Techniques for Risk Management 74

9.3 Identifying and Mitigating Risks 75

9.4 Continual Risk Evaluation 76

9.5 Creating a Risk Management Plan 78

Chapter 10: Preparing for Cyber Incidents 79

10.1 Steps to Prepare for a Cyber Incident 79

10.2 Creating an Incident Response Plan 80

10.3 The Importance of Regular Plan Updates 81

- 10.4 Simulation and Training 82
- 10.5 Responding to a Cyber Incident 84

Chapter 11: Emerging Technologies and Future Threats 85
- 11.1 Summary of Up-and-Coming Cybersecurity Technologies 85
- 11.2 Predictions on Future Cyber Threats 86
- 11.3 Preparing for AI and Machine Learning in Cybersecurity 87
- 11.4 The Role of Blockchain in Security 88

Chapter 12: Continuing Your Cybersecurity Education 90
- 12.1 Resources for Further Learning 90
- 12.2 Cybersecurity Courses and Certifications 91
- 12.3 Building a Career in Cybersecurity 92
- 12.4 Staying Current: The Importance of Continuous Learning 93
- 12.5 Networking and Professional Development in Cybersecurity ... 94

Chapter 13: Career Opportunities in Cybersecurity 96
- 13.1 Sector-Wise Demand for Cybersecurity Professionals 96
- 13.2 Emerging Roles in Cybersecurity 97
- 13.3 Navigating the Cybersecurity Job Market 98
- 13.4 Long-Term Career Development in Cybersecurity 99

HERE ARE YOUR FREE GIFTS!

1. **922 CompTIA Security+ Exam Flash Cards**
   Access a comprehensive set of 922 expertly crafted flashcards to help you master the key concepts and prepare for the CompTIA Security+ certification exam. These flashcards cover essential topics and are designed to streamline your study process, giving you the edge you need to succeed.

2. **Cybersecurity Career Planner**
   Begin your journey to a successful career in cybersecurity! This planner offers you step-by-step guidance, actionable tips, and valuable resources to help you navigate the rapidly growing field of cybersecurity, ensuring you make informed and strategic career decisions.

3. **Incident Response Checklist**
   Equip yourself with our exclusive Incident Response Checklist to handle cyberattacks efficiently and effectively. This tool provides you with a structured approach to managing incidents, minimizing damage, and recovering quickly from security breaches.

SCAN HERE TO DOWNLOAD YOUR GIFTS!

Chapter 1: Introduction to Cybersecurity

1.1 What is Cybersecurity?

The practice and procedures involved in defending computers, servers, mobile devices, electronic systems, networks, and data from hostile attacks are collectively referred to as cybersecurity. It includes a variety of disciplines designed to protect assets from harm, cyberattacks, and unlawful access. As our reliance on technology deepens, the scope of cybersecurity extends beyond traditional IT sectors, impacting almost every aspect of modern life where digital infrastructure is involved.

The field is broad and multifaceted, dealing with various forms of cyber threats such as viruses, worms, spyware, ransomware, and phishing attacks. Cybersecurity measures are essential to prevent attackers from exploiting vulnerabilities to infiltrate and potentially cripple networks, steal sensitive data, or disrupt services. This field is not just about defending against threats, but also about developing an ongoing, adaptive security strategy that evolves with new technologies and tactics used by cybercriminals.

At its core, cybersecurity involves three primary areas of security:

- **Physical security:** Making sure that IT assets, such as data centers and hardware, are physically protected.
- **Network security**: Protecting data in transit via networks by employing secure protocols such as SSL/TLS and more.
- **Information security**: Safeguarding data integrity and privacy in storage and processing.

Effective cybersecurity strategies often employ a layered approach, sometimes known as "defense in depth," which incorporates multiple levels of security controls within a company. These strategies are not solely technical but also involve administrative and operational aspects, aiming to protect information from a wide spectrum of risks across all layers of the organization.

Moreover, the foundational ideas of cybersecurity are availability, confidentiality, and integrity—commonly referred to as the "CIA triad." Sensitive material must be kept secret and shared only with those who are permitted, according to confidentiality. Integrity ensures information is accurate and unaltered during its lifecycle. Availability guarantees that authorized users can access the data and resources when needed.

As we delve deeper into the digital age, cybersecurity's role continues to grow, not only in its traditional realms but also in new sectors such as cloud computing, artificial intelligence, and Internet of Things (IoT) devices, each bringing unique vulnerabilities and challenges.

1.2 Cybersecurity's Significance in the Modern World

The importance of cybersecurity in the linked world of today cannot be emphasized. It plays a crucial role in protecting personal, corporate, and national assets from high-stakes threats, making it an indispensable part of our digital lives. As we increasingly depend on digital technologies for everything from commerce and communication to governance and healthcare, the potential impact of cyber threats also escalates.

Economic Impact: Cybersecurity is vital for protecting the economic stability of individuals, companies, and nations. Cyberattacks can lead to direct financial losses from theft of banking information, payment card fraud, and disruption of trading. Beyond these immediate losses, there are costs related to repairing affected systems, strengthening security post-attack, and potential legal liabilities associated with breaches of sensitive customer information. For businesses, a significant cyberattack can also result in a loss of consumer trust and damage to brand reputation, which can have long-lasting financial consequences.

Infrastructure and National Security: Critical infrastructure sectors such as energy, transportation, and utilities rely heavily on digital systems to operate efficiently. Attacks on these systems can lead to catastrophic consequences, disrupting essential services and potentially leading to national emergencies. For governments, cybersecurity is a priority for national defense, as it protects information related to national security and prevents espionage and sabotage by hostile entities.

Privacy Protection: With the vast amounts of personal data stored online, protecting privacy has become a primary concern of cybersecurity. Individuals rely on cybersecurity measures to protect personal information from being stolen and misused. Privacy breaches can lead to identity theft, financial loss, and personal embarrassment or harm.

Regulatory Compliance: For many industries, cybersecurity is also about compliance with regulations designed to protect the privacy and integrity of data. Cybersecurity is a crucial component of legal compliance because of the strict regulations on data processing and privacy imposed by laws like the California Consumer Privacy Act (CCPA) in the US and the General Data Protection Regulation (GDPR) in the EU.

Adaptation to Evolving Threats: Cybersecurity is significant not only because of the current threats but also due to the ever-evolving nature of risks as technology advances. Cybersecurity professionals must continuously learn and adapt to new threats posed by emerging technologies like artificial intelligence and the Internet of Things (IoT). Each new technology brings unique vulnerabilities, and cybersecurity strategies must evolve accordingly to address these challenges.

Enabler of Innovation: Secure environments are a prerequisite for technological innovation. Companies and developers are more likely to innovate when they know their systems are secure from theft and sabotage. Cybersecurity, therefore, not only protects existing systems but also fosters an environment where innovation can flourish.

The significance of cybersecurity is thus rooted in its capacity to protect and enable society in a variety of ways. It is a dynamic field that requires constant vigilance and adaptation to protect against known threats and prepare for future challenges. As the digital landscape grows, so does the role of cybersecurity in shaping a safe and stable future.

1.3 Common Misconceptions about Cybersecurity

Cybersecurity is a field surrounded by many myths and misconceptions that can affect how individuals and organizations approach their security strategies. Here are some of the most common misconceptions and the realities behind them:

Misconception 1: Small Businesses Are Not Targets Many small to medium-sized enterprises (SMEs) believe they're not targets for cyberattacks because they don't have as many assets as large corporations. The reality is quite the opposite. Small businesses are often seen as easy targets because they typically invest less in their cybersecurity defenses, making them vulnerable to attacks. In fact, a significant percentage of cyberattacks are aimed at small businesses due to their weaker security measures and the easier access to larger networks through vendor connections.

Misconception 2: Cybersecurity Is Solely an IT Issue While IT teams play a crucial role in implementing and maintaining cybersecurity measures, cybersecurity is a responsibility that spans across all departments of an organization. Human error is one of the largest contributors to security breaches, and employees outside of the IT department can often be the weakest links, making education and awareness across all levels and departments essential for a robust cybersecurity posture.

Misconception 3: Strong Passwords Are Sufficient Protection While strong passwords are an important part of cybersecurity defenses, they are not enough on their own. Cyber attackers have sophisticated tools and techniques at their disposal, such as phishing attacks and advanced malware, which can bypass password protections. Multifactor authentication, regular software updates, and other security measures are also necessary to protect against a wide array of threats.

Misconception 4: Cybersecurity Is Too Expensive Many organizations, especially small ones, view cybersecurity as a costly endeavor. However, the cost of preventing attacks is typically much lower than the cost of dealing with a data breach, which includes legal fees, fines, remediation costs, and damage to reputation. In the long run, investing in cybersecurity makes financial sense given the possible costs from a cyber attack.

Misconception 5: Once Secure, Always Secure Some believe that once they have implemented a cybersecurity solution, no further action is needed. This overlooks the dynamic nature of cyber threats. Cybersecurity requires continuous improvement and regular updates to defense mechanisms. Threats evolve rapidly, and cybersecurity measures must adapt just as quickly to address new vulnerabilities and attack methods.

Misconception 6: Antivirus Software is Enough to Keep an Organization Safe While antivirus software is a necessary tool in the cybersecurity arsenal, relying solely on it is insufficient. Modern cyber threats are multifaceted and require a combination of strategies including firewalls, intrusion detection systems, data encryption, and more comprehensive monitoring and response strategies.

Misconception 7: Cyberattacks are Always Obvious Many users expect a cyberattack to be immediately obvious, like a crashed system or a ransom note. However, many sophisticated attacks are designed to be stealthy and can remain undetected for long periods. Regular system audits and continuous monitoring are essential for detecting these hidden threats.

1.4 How Cybersecurity Affects You

Cybersecurity impacts virtually every aspect of our digital lives, often in ways we may not readily perceive. Understanding how cybersecurity affects individuals, businesses, and society as a whole can help underscore the importance of maintaining robust security practices. Here's a closer look at these impacts:

For Individuals:

1. **Privacy Protection:** Cybersecurity measures are critical to protect personal information from unauthorized access and theft. This includes financial data, health records, personal emails, and other sensitive information that, if exposed, could lead to identity theft or financial fraud.

2. **Safe Online Transactions:** Reliable cybersecurity measures like encryption and secure payment gateways are essential for safe online banking and shopping. Without these protections, your financial information and personal data could be at risk every time you make a transaction.

3. **Social Media Security:** Cybersecurity also plays a vital role in protecting your social media accounts from hacking and misuse. This not only protects personal information but also helps prevent malicious activities conducted from hijacked accounts.

For Businesses:

1. **Operational Continuity**: Robust cybersecurity makes it possible for companies to run without being disrupted by cyberattacks. This includes protection against ransomware, DDoS attacks, and other threats that can disrupt operations and cause significant downtime.

2. **Protection of Intellectual Property:** Businesses invest heavily in intellectual property, which can include proprietary software, business strategies, and trade secrets. Cybersecurity measures protect these assets from industrial espionage and theft.

3. **Regulatory Compliance:** Many businesses operate under regulations that require them to protect customer data, such as GDPR or HIPAA. Cybersecurity practices ensure compliance with these regulations, avoiding potential legal penalties and fines.

For Society:

1. **National Security:** Cybersecurity is crucial for protecting a country's critical infrastructure—including power grids, water systems, and transportation networks—from cyberattacks that could cause widespread chaos and danger to public safety.

2. **Economic Stability:** By safeguarding businesses and infrastructure, cybersecurity contributes to the overall economic stability and growth. Cyberattacks can have severe economic implications by undermining business confidence, causing stock market fluctuations, and imposing heavy costs on both public and private sectors.

3. **Trust in Digital Systems:** Robust cybersecurity measures build trust in digital systems, encouraging the adoption and development of new technologies like the Internet of Things (IoT), artificial intelligence, and more. This trust is crucial for the advancement of digital transformation in society.

Personal Impact: Cybersecurity directly affects how safe you feel using digital technologies and the internet. When cybersecurity measures are strong, you can engage more confidently in the digital world. Conversely, weak cybersecurity can make you vulnerable to cyber threats, impacting your online freedom and security.

1.5 Key Terms and Concepts in Cybersecurity

Cybersecurity is filled with specific terms and concepts that are essential to understanding how to protect systems and data effectively. Here's an overview of some of the fundamental terms and concepts that anyone interested in cybersecurity should know:

1. **Malware**: Malware, an acronym for "malicious software," is any application or file that poses a risk to computer users. Malware can take the form of ransomware, worms, Trojan horses, and viruses. Every variety can harm data and systems to differing degrees and infects differently.

2. **Phishing**: This kind of social engineering approach is frequently employed to obtain credit card details and login passwords from users. It occurs when an attacker pretending to be a trustworthy source tricks a victim into opening an email, text message, or instant message.

3. **Ransomware**: This refers to a type of malicious software designed to block users' access to a computer system until a specific sum of money is paid. Drive-by downloads and phishing emails with infected files are two common ways that ransomware spreads.

4. **Firewall**: A firewall acts as a gatekeeper for network traffic, scrutinizing both incoming and outgoing data to determine if it meets specified security criteria before allowing or blocking its passage. It serves as a crucial barrier between trusted internal networks and potentially harmful external networks, like the Internet.

5. **Encryption**: Encryption involves transforming information into a coded format, primarily to prevent unauthorized access. This process is vital for safeguarding sensitive data during transmission over networks or while stored on various devices.

6. **Intrusion Detection System (IDS)** and **Intrusion Prevention System (IPS)**: These tools are designed to identify and potentially thwart network breaches. IDS keeps a watchful eye for suspicious behavior, issuing alerts upon detecting potential threats, while IPS actively blocks such threats based on predefined security protocols.

7. **Virtual Private Network (VPN)**: VPN broadens the scope of a private network over a public one, enabling users to securely share data across shared or public networks as if they were directly linked to the private network. By doing so, it enhances online privacy and anonymity by establishing a secure tunnel within the public internet.

8. **Zero-Day Exploit**: Zero-Day Exploits refer to vulnerabilities in software that remain unknown to the vendor. Hackers exploit these security gaps before the vendor can address them, earning the name "zero-day" because they occur before any protective measures are in place.

9. **Botnet**: A Botnet is a network of compromised computers infected with malicious software, controlled collectively without their owners' awareness. Botnets are commonly utilized for activities such as disseminating spam messages or launching cyber attacks.

10. **DDoS Attack**: Distributed Denial of Service attacks, also known as DDoS attacks, aim to disrupt the normal operation of a targeted server, service, or network by overwhelming it with an excessive volume of internet traffic. This flood of data overwhelms the target and its surrounding infrastructure, rendering them inaccessible to legitimate users.

11. **Two-Factor Authentication (2FA)**: In order to confirm their identity, users using Two-Factor Authentication (2FA) must supply two unique authentication factors. This method enhances security by protecting both user credentials and the resources they are attempting to access.

12. **Cybersecurity Hygiene**: Cybersecurity Hygiene encompasses the practices and measures users implement to uphold system integrity and bolster online security. These routines are typically integrated into regular activities to safeguard identity, data, and networks.

Chapter 2: Understanding Cyber Threats

2.1 Types of Cyber Threats

Recognizing the different types of cyber threats is essential for devising effective defense strategies. Cyber threats manifest in various forms, each targeting specific weaknesses or aiming for particular malicious goals. Below are some of the most prevalent cyber threats:

1. **Viruses and Worms:** These are among the oldest cyber threats. Viruses attach themselves to clean files, spreading to other computers, while worms self-replicate without needing a host program. They commonly exploit operating system vulnerabilities.

2. **Trojan Horses:** This malware masquerades as legitimate software. Unlike viruses and worms, Trojans don't propagate by infecting other files or self-replicate. Instead, they're utilized to pilfer information or create entry points for additional malware.

3. **Ransomware:** This malware encrypts or locks data, demanding payment for data access restoration. Ransomware incidents have surged, targeting sectors like healthcare, education, and government.

4. **Phishing:** In this scheme, deceptive communications, often via email, mimic reputable sources to steal sensitive data or install malware on victims' devices.

5. **Spyware:** Designed covertly, spyware gathers information without user consent, including personal conversations, passwords, and financial details.

6. **Adware:** Often bundled with free software, adware tracks browsing activities and downloads to display ads. While not inherently malicious, some adware can severely impact system performance and security.

7. **Spam:** The digital equivalent of junk mail, spam isn't directly harmful but can serve as a conduit for malware delivery.

8. **Man-in-the-Middle (MitM) Attacks:** Attackers insert themselves into two-party transactions to intercept and pilfer data, especially concerning on unsecured WiFi networks and during online financial transactions.

9. **Denial-of-Service (DoS) and Distributed Denial of Service (DDoS) Attacks:** These assaults aim to render a machine or network inaccessible by inundating them with traffic. DoS attacks exhaust resources, while DDoS attacks involve multiple sources targeting a victim, posing greater defense challenges.

10. **SQL Injection:** Hackers inject malicious code into SQL to manipulate a web application's database server, potentially accessing, altering, or deleting data.

11. **Zero-Day Exploits:** Hackers exploit unknown vulnerabilities in software or hardware before developers can patch them, posing significant risks due to the lack of available defenses.

12. **Drive-by Downloads:** These attacks surreptitiously download malware onto users' systems when they visit compromised or malicious websites, often without their consent.

2.1.1 Viruses and Worms

Viruses and worms represent some of the oldest and most conventional types of malware, posing persistent threats to computer systems over decades. Despite their shared capacity to spread and cause harm, they operate uniquely, carrying distinct implications for cybersecurity.

Viruses:

1. **Propagation Method:** Viruses are code fragments that affix themselves to legitimate programs or documents (referred to as hosts), necessitating human action to replicate, typically through opening files or executing programs. Upon activation, they can infiltrate other files or programs, perpetuating their dissemination.

2. **Effects:** Viruses exhibit a wide range of effects, from mere annoyance, such as displaying messages or images, to severe damage like data corruption, hard drive reformatting, or security software incapacitation. They may also establish system security backdoors, facilitating further exploitation.

3. **Examples:** Renowned instances of viruses include the ILOVEYOU virus, which proliferated via email, impacting millions of computers globally and resulting in billions of dollars in damages through file overwrites.

Worms:

1. **Propagation Method:** Worms are autonomous malware entities that do not rely on host file attachment. Exploiting system or software vulnerabilities, they traverse networks, often without human intervention. Worms can proliferate rapidly and extensively.

2. **Effects:** Primarily, worms disrupt networks by consuming bandwidth and overloading web servers, leading to network performance degradation or cessation. They can also deploy payloads enabling attackers to manipulate compromised systems, pilfer data, or introduce additional malware.

3. **Examples:** Notorious among worm instances is the Conficker worm, which leveraged Microsoft Windows vulnerabilities to infect millions of computers, enlisting them into a criminal botnet.

Prevention and Mitigation: • **Antivirus and Antimalware Software:** These constitute initial defense layers, necessitating regular updates to identify and eradicate malicious programs. • **Regular Updates and Patches:** Vital for maintaining system integrity, regular updates and patch installations are crucial. Many worms exploit known vulnerabilities for which patches exist but remain unimplemented by users. • **Good Security Practices:** Practices like abstaining from opening unexpected email attachments, refraining from downloading software from dubious sources, and exercising caution when clicking on email or online links are imperative. • **Network Security Measures:** Employing firewalls and intrusion detection systems aids in thwarting worm propagation across networks. • **Education and Awareness:** Users should be informed about the risks associated with opening unfamiliar attachments or clicking on suspicious links, even from seemingly familiar contacts.

2.1.2 Trojan Horses

Trojan horses, or simply "Trojans," are a type of malware that are particularly deceptive in nature, as they disguise themselves as legitimate software. Unlike viruses and worms, Trojans do not replicate themselves but are equally dangerous due to their capability to provide a backdoor for additional malicious actions.

Mechanics of Trojans:

1. **Deceptive Appearance**: Trojans masquerade as useful, legitimate software, enticing users to download and install them. This disguise can vary from seemingly harmless applications to software updates and utility tools.

2. **Execution**: Once installed, a Trojan can perform a range of malicious activities. These activities can be directly harmful, such as deleting or modifying data, or they can involve more covert actions, such as spying on the user's activities and silently gathering sensitive information.

3. **Distribution**: Trojans can be distributed through various channels. Common methods include email attachments, downloadable software from untrusted websites, or via other compromised software.

Types of Trojans:

- **Backdoor Trojans**: These create a "backdoor" on a user's computer, allowing an attacker to gain remote control over the infected machine, often leading to a loss of data or further malware infections.

- **Exploit Trojans**: They contain data or code that exploits a vulnerability in the software running on your computer.

- **Rootkit Trojans**: These are designed to hide certain objects or activities in your system, often making the Trojan difficult to detect and remove.

- **Banker Trojans**: These are specifically designed to steal sensitive information used for online banking and financial transactions.

- **DDoS Trojans**: These convert the affected computers into bots that can be used to perform distributed denial-of-service (DDoS) attacks on targeted networks.

Impact of Trojans:

- **Security Breach**: Trojans can lead to significant security breaches, allowing cybercriminals to access your personal information, financial data, and even hijack your computer's resources.

- **Data Loss**: Some Trojans are designed to delete or corrupt data, which can be particularly devastating for individuals or businesses.

- **System Damage**: Trojans may cause your system to become unstable or unusable, requiring a full reinstall and potential loss of data.

Prevention and Mitigation:

- **Antivirus and Anti-Malware Programs**: Installing and maintaining updated antivirus software can detect and remove Trojans before they cause harm.

- **Software Updates**: Keeping your operating system and applications up-to-date reduces vulnerabilities that Trojans might exploit.

- **User Vigilance**: Avoid downloading and installing software from untrusted sources, be wary of email attachments, and always verify the authenticity of the software by checking digital signatures or publisher details.
- **Network Security**: Using firewalls and other security protocols can help prevent unauthorized access and block communications with malicious sources.

2.1.3 Ransomware

A particularly vicious type of malware is called ransomware, which encrypts a victim's files and holds them captive until a ransom is paid. This kind of cyberattack, which targets people, companies, and even government organizations, is becoming more common and sophisticated.

How Ransomware Works:

1. **Infection**: Ransomware can infect systems through various methods, including phishing emails, malicious advertisements, and exploiting vulnerabilities in software. Once executed on a system, the ransomware will typically scan for valuable files, including documents, databases, and personal photos, and encrypt them using strong cryptographic algorithms.
2. **Demand**: After the files are encrypted, ransomware displays a message demanding a ransom, usually in cryptocurrencies such as Bitcoin, to provide an anonymous way to receive payment. The ransom note explains how to pay the ransom and often includes a deadline after which the decryption key will allegedly be destroyed if payment isn't made.
3. **Decryption**: The attackers promise to provide a decryption key to unlock the files once the ransom is paid. However, paying the ransom does not guarantee that the files will be decrypted; there are many instances where organizations or individuals have paid the ransom and either did not receive a key or received a key that didn't work.

Types of Ransomware:

- **Encrypting Ransomware**: This is the most prevalent type, encrypting the victim's files and requesting a ransom to unlock them.
- **Locker Ransomware**: Locker ransomware is different from encrypting ransomware in that it locks the victim out of their device, preventing them from accessing any contents.
- **Scareware**: This type of pseudo-ransomware uses scare tactics to trick victims into paying money to resolve non-existent problems, such as fake antivirus messages claiming that malware has been detected and requires payment to clean.

Impact of Ransomware:

- **Operational Disruption**: For businesses, ransomware can paralyze entire operations, leading to significant financial losses due to downtime and lost productivity.
- **Financial Loss**: Beyond the ransom payments, victims often incur additional costs in response efforts, such as forensic analysis, data recovery, and enhancing security post-attack.

- **Reputational Damage**: Organizations suffering from ransomware attacks may also experience a loss of trust from customers and partners, which can be damaging in the long term.

Prevention and Mitigation:

- **Data Backup Strategy:** Regularly backing up data and ensuring its accessibility and security stands as the most potent measure to mitigate the impact of ransomware attacks. It's imperative to store these backups separately from the network to prevent potential encryption.
- **Employee Training on Security Awareness:** Educating staff about the dangers posed by phishing and other infection vectors can lower the probability of ransomware infiltrations.
- **System Patching and Updates:** Maintaining current versions of operating systems and software is crucial for closing security loopholes that ransomware exploits.
- **Utilization of Antivirus and Anti-Malware Solutions:** Employing robust security solutions can frequently identify and isolate ransomware before it executes its harmful actions.
- **Development of Incident Response Plans:** Establishing a protocol for addressing ransomware attacks enables organizations to swiftly recover operations and limit associated damages.

2.1.4 Phishing

Phishing is a type of social engineering assault that is frequently used to get credit card numbers and login passwords from users. This type of attack involves deceiving the victims into believing that they are interacting with a trusted party, such as their bank, a major online retailer, or a widely used service, in order to trick them into divulging confidential information.

How Phishing Works:

1. **Deceptive Communication:** Phishing attempts frequently commence with a message crafted to mimic a trusted source, such as an email, text, social media post, or any digital correspondence the recipient is inclined to trust.
2. **Urgent or Tempting Messages:** These messages typically convey a sense of urgency or offer enticing incentives to induce immediate action. They may include alarming alerts regarding account security threats, promises of refunds, reports of unauthorized access, or seemingly irresistible giveaways.
3. **Malicious Links or Attachments:** Such messages often feature harmful links or attachments capable of stealing personal data or infecting the user's device with malware. These links might redirect users to counterfeit websites resembling legitimate ones, where any submitted information is directly transmitted to the attackers.

Types of Phishing:

- **Spear Phishing**: Unlike random, broad-spectrum phishing attacks, spear phishing targets specific individuals or organizations. These attacks are often more dangerous because they are highly tailored to their victims, using more personalized details to seem legitimate.
- **Whaling**: This phishing variant targets prominent individuals like senior executives. The content is meticulously crafted to align with high-stakes corporate dealings, enhancing the credibility of fraudulent communications.

- **Smishing and Vishing**: Smishing employs SMS for phishing messages, while vishing uses voice calls. Both exploit personal interactions to pilfer confidential information.

Impact of Phishing:

- **Identity Theft**: Phishing can lead to significant personal data loss, resulting in identity theft.
- **Financial Loss**: For individuals and organizations alike, phishing can result in direct financial loss through fraudulent transactions or the stealing of financial information.
- **Access to Broader Networks**: Gaining access to one person's credentials can allow attackers to infiltrate an organization's entire network, leading to broader security breaches.

Prevention and Mitigation:

- **User Education and Training:** Conducting regular training sessions for employees on identifying and responding to phishing attempts is essential.
- **Advanced Email Filtering:** Employing tools to filter out phishing emails before reaching user inboxes can diminish the likelihood of attacks.
- **Verification of Contacts:** When messages request sensitive information or prompt immediate action, verifying authenticity through official channels is crucial.
- **Multi-Factor Authentication (MFA):** MFA adds an extra security layer by necessitating more than just a password for access, mitigating unauthorized access risks even if credentials are compromised.
- **Regular System Updates and Patching:** Keeping software and systems up to date can help prevent attackers from exploiting known vulnerabilities.

2.1.5 Spyware

Spyware is a type of malware designed to secretly monitor and collect personal or organizational information. It is covert in nature and can be used to track everything from personal browsing habits to confidential corporate data without the knowledge or consent of the user.

How Spyware Works:

1. **Invasion and Installation**: Spyware typically enters a system through bundled software installations, deceptive links, email attachments, or as a payload of another malware. Once installed, it remains hidden from the user and operates silently in the background.

2. **Data Collection**: Spyware can record a variety of data types including keystrokes, browsing history, login credentials, and financial information. More sophisticated spyware can capture screenshots, activate cameras, and record audio from the device.

3. **Data Transmission**: The collected data is usually sent to a remote attacker or organization who can use it for various malicious purposes, such as identity theft, fraud, or corporate espionage.

Types of Spyware:

- **Keyloggers**: These programs log all computer keystrokes, making it possible for hackers to obtain private data including credit card numbers, usernames, and passwords.

- **Adware**: Often considered a less malicious form of spyware, adware tracks a user's browsing habits to display targeted advertising. However, it can degrade system performance and security.

- **Trojan Spyware**: This type of spyware is hidden within seemingly legitimate software and, once activated, can steal information or spy on the user.

- **System Monitors**: These are comprehensive monitoring tools that can log virtually everything done on a computer—applications used, websites visited, chats, emails, and more.

Impact of Spyware:

- **Privacy Violation**: Spyware infringes on personal privacy and can lead to significant security issues for individuals and organizations, leading to a loss of confidential or proprietary information.

- **Resource Consumption**: Spyware can slow down systems and reduce the efficiency of network connections by consuming bandwidth and processing power.

- **Legal and Reputational Damage**: For businesses, spyware can lead to legal repercussions if sensitive customer data is compromised, as well as significant reputational damage.

Prevention and Mitigation:

- **Anti-Spyware and Antivirus Software**: Installing and regularly updating reputable anti-spyware and antivirus software can help detect and remove spyware.

- **Practicing Safe Browsing:** Refrain from clicking on unfamiliar links or downloading software from sources lacking reliability. Utilize web browser configurations that inhibit pop-ups and disallow unauthorized downloads.

- **Frequent Software Updates:** Maintaining up-to-date software across all facets, including the operating system and applications, serves as a deterrent against spyware exploiting vulnerabilities.
- **Enhanced Network Security:** Employ firewalls and network security mechanisms to oversee and regulate both incoming and outgoing network traffic, effectively thwarting unauthorized data transfers.
- **Educational Initiatives and Awareness:** Conduct training sessions, particularly within organizational environments, to enlighten users about the perils of spyware and underscore the significance of adhering to established security protocols.

2.1.6 Adware

Adware, also known as advertising-supported software, is a category of malware designed to distribute advertisements automatically. Typically, it's utilized by software developers as a means to generate income by integrating ads into their software. Nevertheless, when manifested in malicious forms, adware can significantly disrupt user experience, degrade system performance, and infringe upon user privacy.

How Adware Works:

1. **Distribution**: Adware can be installed on a system through bundled software where users unwittingly install it alongside legitimate software. It can also be downloaded by clicking on malicious links or ads, or as a payload delivered by other malware.
2. **Operation**: Once installed, adware begins delivering ads in various forms—pop-ups, banners, or unauthorized changes to browser settings (like changing your homepage or default search engine). These ads are often intrusive and can significantly disrupt the user experience.
3. **Monetization**: The primary motive behind adware is to generate revenue through ad views and clicks. Malicious adware may also collect data on browsing habits and personal preferences to target ads more effectively, which can lead to privacy breaches.

Types of Adware:

- **Browser Hijackers**: This type of adware redirects your browser traffic to certain websites, often changing your default homepage and search engine to ones controlled by the adware.
- **Popup Adware**: As the name suggests, this adware generates numerous popup ads on your screen, which can be difficult to close and may reappear persistently.
- **Legitimate Ad-supported Software**: Not all adware is malicious. Some legitimate applications use advertising as a way to offer free versions of their software. These ads are usually displayed in a non-intrusive manner.

Impact of Adware:

- **Degraded System Performance**: Adware can consume system resources (CPU, memory), slowing down the computer and affecting its overall performance.
- **Compromised User Experience**: Constant advertisements can be a major disruption during normal computer use, affecting productivity and usability.

- **Privacy Concerns**: Since some adware tracks user activity and collects data, there is a significant risk of privacy infringement, particularly if this information is shared with third parties without user consent.

Prevention and Mitigation:

- **Employ Trusted Antivirus and Anti-Adware Software**: These tools are often capable of identifying and eliminating adware before it inflicts harm.

- **Source Software from Reliable Channels**: Refrain from downloading programs from unfamiliar sources; instead, opt for official websites or reputable vendors.

- **Exercise Caution During Installation**: Many adware instances are bundled with other software. Pay close attention to installation prompts and decline any offers for additional software or suspicious applications.

- **Maintain Regular Software Updates**: Ensure all software, particularly web browsers and operating systems, remain updated to mitigate vulnerabilities exploited by adware.

- **Utilize Ad Blockers**: Installing ad blockers can prevent various types of adware from displaying advertisements, providing an added layer of defense against potentially harmful ads.

2.1.7 Spam

Spam refers to unsolicited digital messages, usually sent in bulk and often containing advertisements, phishing attempts, or other potentially harmful content. Originally limited primarily to email, spam now proliferates across various digital platforms, including instant messaging, social media, and mobile texts.

How Spam Works:

1. **Distribution**: Spam is distributed in large volumes to numerous recipients, often using automated tools that can send thousands of messages very quickly. These messages are typically generated from lists of collected or purchased email addresses and other contact information.

2. **Content Variety**: The content of spam messages can vary widely but commonly includes promotions for dubious products, links to malware-infected websites, or attempts to elicit personal information under false pretenses.

3. **Economic Motive**: Most spam is sent with the goal of economic gain—either through direct sales of products or services, by phishing for sensitive information that can be used in fraudulent activities, or through pay-per-click schemes where senders earn money based on the number of people who click links within the spam messages.

Types of Spam:

- **Commercial Spam**: This includes unsolicited promotional emails for products and services. While some might be merely annoying, others can be deceptive or link to fraudulent websites.

- **Phishing Emails**: A dangerous type of spam that tries to trick recipients into providing sensitive personal information by masquerading as legitimate communication from banks, service providers, or well-known companies.

- **Malware Spam**: These emails contain or link to malicious software designed to harm the recipient's system or to steal information.
- **Social Media Spam**: This type can appear as unwanted comments, posts, or direct messages on social media platforms, often promoting scams, misleading information, or links to harmful sites.

Impact of Spam:

- **Reduced Productivity**: Sorting through and deleting spam emails can consume valuable time, reducing individual and organizational productivity.
- **Security Risks**: Spam often carries malware or phishing links that can lead to significant security breaches.
- **Resource Drain**: Managing spam can drain network and email server resources, affecting the performance of IT systems.

Prevention and Mitigation:

- **Spam Filters**: Utilize advanced spam filters that can be configured to recognize and block spam messages based on their source, content, and other attributes.
- **Best Email Practices**: Steer clear of opening questionable emails, clicking on unfamiliar links, or downloading attachments from sources lacking trustworthiness.
- **User Education**: Train users to recognize spam and understand the risks associated with interacting with spam messages.
- **Regular Updates and Patches**: Keeping systems and software updated helps protect against vulnerabilities that spammers might exploit.
- **Reporting Spam**: Many platforms allow users to report spam. This not only helps remove the spam from your interface but also aids service providers in improving their spam detection mechanisms.

2.1.8 Man-in-the-Middle (MitM) Attacks

Man-in-the-Middle (MitM) attacks represent a cybersecurity menace wherein the attacker clandestinely intercepts and potentially modifies the communication between two parties who perceive they are communicating directly. This enables the attacker to eavesdrop on the interaction and manipulate the transmitted information without the sender or recipient detecting the intrusion.

How MitM Attacks Work:

1. **Interception**: The first step in a MitM attack involves the attacker positioning themselves in a network position that allows them to intercept messages between the sender and receiver. This can be achieved through various techniques such as packet sniffing on unsecured networks, IP spoofing, or DNS spoofing.

2. **Decryption (if necessary)**: If the communications are encrypted, sophisticated attackers might use methods like SSL stripping to downgrade the connection to a non-secure version, or they might use stolen encryption keys to decrypt the messages.

3. **Data Manipulation**: Once the data is intercepted, the attacker can alter it before passing it along to the recipient, thereby deceiving the parties and manipulating the communication to their advantage.

4. **Transmission**: After interception and potential alteration, the attacker sends the fraudulent or altered data to the receiving party, who remains unaware of the compromise.

Types of MitM Attacks:

- **Wi-Fi Eavesdropping**: Occurs when an attacker sets up a rogue Wi-Fi network or compromises an existing one to intercept data transmitted by users connected to the network.

- **Session Hijacking**: Involves stealing a session token to gain unauthorized access to a web service or application after a user has authenticated themselves.

- **SSL Stripping**: The attacker forces a connection to revert from HTTPS (secure) to HTTP (non-secure) in order to intercept data that can then be transmitted in plain text.

- **Email Hijacking**: Attackers illicitly acquire access to an email account, monitoring transactions and data exchanges to pilfer sensitive information or engage in fraudulent activities.

Impact of MitM Attacks:

- **Loss of Confidential Information**: Personal and sensitive data like login credentials, credit card numbers, and corporate information are susceptible to theft.

- **Financial Fraud**: Manipulated communication can lead to unauthorized financial transactions.

- **Loss of Trust**: Both personal and professional relationships can suffer if sensitive or private communications are disclosed or manipulated.

Prevention and Mitigation:

- **Utilize Encryption**: Employ robust encryption protocols like HTTPS to safeguard data during transit.

- **Secure Wi-Fi Connections**: Refrain from conducting sensitive transactions over public Wi-Fi networks, or employ a reputable VPN to encrypt data transmission on such networks.

- **Implement Multi-Factor Authentication**: Utilize multi-factor authentication to thwart unauthorized access even if credentials are compromised in a MitM attack.

- **Maintain Software Updates**: Regularly update software and hardware to mitigate known vulnerabilities that could be exploited in MitM attacks.

- **Promote Education and Awareness**: Educate users about the dangers of MitM attacks and advocate for best practices, including verifying website authenticity and scrutinizing digital communications for signs of tampering.

2.1.9 DoS and DDoS Attacks

Denial of Service (DoS) and Distributed Denial of Service (DDoS) attacks are common cyber threats designed to disrupt the regular operations of targeted resources. Through inundating the target with a deluge of internet traffic, these attacks can incapacitate websites, services, or networks, rendering them inaccessible to legitimate users.

How DoS and DDoS Attacks Work:

1. **Volume of Traffic**: In a DoS attack, a single internet connection is used to flood a target with bogus requests, intended to overload the system. A DDoS attack amplifies this by utilizing multiple compromised devices (often part of a botnet) to launch the massive flood of traffic simultaneously, vastly increasing the attack's scale and effectiveness.

2. **Exploitation of Network Vulnerabilities**: These attacks can also exploit specific network vulnerabilities to multiply their impact, such as amplification attacks where the attacker sends small requests to a network service, which then responds with a much larger reply.

3. **Resource Exhaustion**: Both types of attacks aim to exhaust the resources on the targeted network or service (such as bandwidth, server processing capacity, or memory), thereby denying service to legitimate users.

Types of DoS/DDoS Attacks:

- **Volume-based Attacks**: These encompass ICMP floods, UDP floods, and other spoofed-packet floods. The objective is to overwhelm the bandwidth of the targeted site, with size gauged in bits per second (Bps).

- **Application Layer Attacks**: These assaults focus on applications, aiming to disrupt the web server. Their intensity is measured in requests per second (Rps).

- **Protocol Attacks**: These involve SYN floods, fragmented packet attacks, Ping of Death, and similar methods. They deplete actual server resources or those of intermediary communication devices like firewalls and load balancers, measured in packets per second (Pps).

Impact of DoS/DDoS Attacks:

- **Service Disruption**: This can range from minor annoyance to significant business-level disruption, depending on the target and duration of the attack.

- **Financial Loss**: Businesses can suffer significant financial losses both directly, through lost sales or service availability, and indirectly, through damaged customer trust and repair costs.
- **Reputational Damage**: Repeated or high-profile attacks can erode trust in a company's ability to secure its services, potentially leading to customer attrition.

Prevention and Mitigation:
- **Increased Network Security**: This involves creating robust firewalls and intrusion detection systems that can recognize and filter out attack traffic.
- **Bandwidth Overprovisioning**: Having bandwidth that exceeds the normal peak load can help absorb the increased traffic of a DoS/DDoS attack.
- **Rate Limiting**: This can restrict the number of requests a server will accept over a certain period of time.
- **Redundant Infrastructure**: Distributing network resources across multiple locations can help mitigate the effect of an attack on a single site.
- **DDoS Mitigation Services**: Numerous organizations currently enlist specialized DDoS mitigation services, which have the capability to intercept and sift through malicious traffic prior to its arrival at the target.

2.1.10 SQL Injection

SQL Injection (SQLi) is a common attack technique that exploits vulnerabilities in a database-driven application's software. These attacks manipulate standard SQL queries to execute unauthorized commands, allowing attackers to bypass security measures, access, manipulate, or destroy sensitive data.

How SQL Injection Works:
1. **Exploitation of Vulnerable Input Fields**: The attack usually occurs when user input undergoes inadequate filtration for string literal escape characters or lacks strong typing, leading to unintended execution as SQL commands. This commonly takes place in user input fields like login forms, search boxes, or URLs.
2. **Execution of Malicious SQL Commands**: Once an attacker finds a vulnerable input field, they can insert SQL statements expected to be executed by the database. This can allow attackers to perform tasks such as viewing data they are not normally able to retrieve, manipulating existing data, executing administration operations like shutting down the DBMS, or even issuing commands to the operating system in some cases.
3. **Data Breaches and Unauthorized Actions**: Depending on the rights of the account under which the SQL commands are executed, an attacker could gain a wide range of unauthorized abilities, from data theft to complete control over the data management software.

Types of SQL Injection:

- **In-band SQLi**: This form of SQL injection is the most straightforward, wherein the attacker utilizes the same communication channel to execute the attack and retrieve results.

- **Inferential SQLi (Blind SQLi)**: This attack method might take longer to exploit as it doesn't directly exchange data between the attacker and the application. Instead, it enables the attacker to reconstruct the database by sending payloads and observing the web application's responses and behavior.

- **Out-of-band SQLi**: This form arises when an attacker is unable to utilize the identical channel for both initiating the attack and retrieving information from the database. It depends on the server's ability to initiate DNS or HTTP requests for transmitting data to the attacker.

Impact of SQL Injection:

- **Data Theft**: SQL Injection can lead to significant breaches involving sensitive or personal data, including financial records, personal identifiable information, and proprietary business details.

- **Database Manipulation or Corruption**: Attackers can alter or delete information, potentially causing persistent issues with the content or functionality of a database-driven application.

- **Loss of Confidentiality and Integrity**: Unauthorized viewing and manipulation of data compromise both the confidentiality and integrity of a database system.

Prevention and Mitigation:

- **Utilizing Prepared Statements (Parameterized Queries):** Employing prepared statements alongside parameterized queries stands as one of the most efficient methods to thwart SQL injection. These mechanisms guarantee that the SQL engine distinguishes between the code and the data, preventing any interference of data with the query structure.

- **Escaping All User-Supplied Input**: This process entails modifying user input to neutralize any harmful SQL statements inserted by attackers, rendering them ineffective and treating them as ordinary data.

- **Deploying Web Application Firewalls (WAFs):** WAFs aid in screening out malicious data by employing rules that identify and block common SQL injection patterns.

- **Conducting Regular Security Assessments**: Incorporating both static analysis (reviewing the code without executing the program) and dynamic analysis (evaluating the code through program execution) helps in identifying vulnerabilities before they can be exploited by attackers.

- **Restricting Database Permissions**: Limiting the permissions granted to databases to only essential functions can mitigate the potential consequences of a successful injection attack.

2.1.11 Zero-Day Exploits

Zero-day exploits represent a significant form of cyber threat, capitalizing on vulnerabilities in software or hardware that were previously undisclosed or unknown. Termed "zero-day" because they emerge without any prior public or vendor disclosure, these vulnerabilities afford no time for software or hardware providers to address the issue before exploitation occurs.

How Zero-Day Exploits Work:

1. **Discovery**: Attackers, or occasionally researchers, discover a vulnerability in software or hardware that developers are not yet aware of. This vulnerability could be in operating systems, browsers, applications, or even hardware devices.

2. **Exploitation**: Once the vulnerability is identified, attackers quickly develop and deploy an exploit. This exploit can be used to gain unauthorized access, steal data, or install malware before the vulnerability becomes publicly known and patched.

3. **Spread**: Zero-day exploits can be distributed through various means such as phishing emails, compromised websites, or through the use of another malware. The speed and method of distribution depend on the attacker's objectives and the nature of the exploit.

Types of Zero-Day Exploits:

- **Remote Code Execution (RCE)**: Allows attackers to execute arbitrary code remotely, potentially gaining full control over the affected system.

- **Privilege Escalation**: Enables attackers to gain higher-level permissions on a system or network, often leading to administrative access.

- **Denial of Service (DoS)**: Can crash a system or network, making it unavailable to users.

- **Data Breach/Leak**: Exploits that specifically target data theft, accessing databases, and other sensitive data repositories.

Impact of Zero-Day Exploits:

- **Significant Security Breaches**: Zero-day exploits can lead to major security incidents, including widespread data breaches, espionage, and loss of sensitive or proprietary information.

- **Reputational Damage**: Organizations affected by zero-day exploits can suffer severe reputational damage, resulting in lost trust and potentially significant financial consequences.

- **Operational Disruption**: Exploits that target critical infrastructure or operational technology can cause significant disruptions and may require extensive recovery time.

Prevention and Mitigation:

- **Regular Software Updates**: While zero-day exploits by definition exploit vulnerabilities before they are patched, keeping all software up to date can quickly reduce the window of opportunity once a patch is available.

- **Advanced Threat Detection Systems**: Employing solutions utilizing behavioral analysis and heuristics aids in identifying unusual activities that might indicate a zero-day exploit before specific signatures are identified.

- **Security Awareness Training**: Educating employees on the hazards of suspicious links and unexpected email attachments can diminish the likelihood of a successful exploit delivery.
- **Robust Incident Response Plan**: Having a plan in place that includes immediate isolation of affected systems and rapid deployment of forensic capabilities can minimize the damage.
- **Bug Bounty Programs**: Encouraging white-hat hackers to find and report vulnerabilities can help organizations identify and fix them before they are exploited maliciously.

2.1.12 Drive-by Downloads

Drive-by downloads are a type of cyber attack where malware is unintentionally downloaded onto a user's system without their explicit consent or knowledge. These attacks exploit vulnerabilities in browsers, plugins, and applications to install malicious software simply by visiting a compromised website.

How Drive-by Downloads Work:

1. **Compromised Websites**: Attackers often exploit vulnerabilities in websites to inject malicious code. Sometimes, reputable websites are compromised to serve malware to unsuspecting visitors, while other times, the attackers create malicious sites designed to look legitimate.
2. **Exploiting Vulnerabilities**: The malicious code typically targets vulnerabilities in the web browser or its plugins like Flash, Java, or PDF readers. When a user visits the infected site, the malware automatically and silently exploits these vulnerabilities to download and install itself.
3. **Silent Execution**: Unlike other types of malware that might require the user to run an executable file, drive-by downloads can occur without any user interaction beyond navigating to the infected web page. The malware begins to execute as soon as it is downloaded, often without the user's knowledge.

Types of Malware Spread by Drive-by Downloads:

- **Spyware**: To monitor user actions and collect personal information.
- **Ransomware**: To encrypt user data and demand a ransom for its decryption.
- **Trojans**: To create backdoors into the system that can be exploited by other malware or attackers.
- **Bots**: To add the infected computer to a botnet for use in coordinated attacks, such as DDoS attacks.

Impact of Drive-by Downloads:

- **System Compromise**: The immediate and primary impact is the compromise of the user's computer system, which can be used for a range of malicious activities.
- **Data Theft and Loss**: Malware installed via drive-by downloads can lead to data theft, including sensitive personal and financial information.
- **Resource Exploitation**: Infected systems can be used to mine cryptocurrencies or to launch further attacks, consuming system resources and potentially causing physical damage to devices.

Prevention and Mitigation:

- **Keep Software Updated**: Regular updates to operating systems, browsers, and all plugins can close security vulnerabilities that are often exploited by drive-by downloads.

- **Use Security Software**: Comprehensive antivirus and anti-malware solutions can detect and block malicious downloads before they execute.

- **Configure Browser Settings**: Adjust browser settings to increase security, such as disabling automatic execution of Java, Flash, or other plugins unless explicitly approved.

- **Web Filtering**: Use web filtering technology that blocks access to known malicious websites and monitors web traffic to prevent access to harmful content.

- **Educate Users**: Regularly educate users about the risks of unknown websites and the importance of maintaining security practices like avoiding suspicious links.

2.2 Profile of Cyber Attackers

Understanding the diverse profiles of cyber attackers is crucial for implementing effective cybersecurity measures. Cyber attackers vary widely in their motivations, resources, and levels of sophistication, which can influence their methods and targets. Here are the main types of cyber attackers:

1. Cybercriminals:

- **Motivation**: Financial gain is the primary driver for cybercriminals. They engage in activities like identity theft, online fraud, and ransomware attacks to extort money.
- **Methods**: Phishing, malware, ransomware, and credit card fraud are common tactics.
- **Profile**: This group can range from lone individuals with basic technical skills to highly organized criminal gangs with significant resources.

2. Hacktivists:

- **Motivation**: Hacktivists are driven by social or political objectives, aiming to draw attention to a cause. They target organizations or governments they view as unethical or corrupt.
- **Methods**: Website defacement, data leaks, and denial-of-service attacks are typical hacktivist tools.
- **Profile**: Often, these attackers are part of loosely organized groups that operate collaboratively, such as Anonymous.

3. State-Sponsored Attackers:

- **Motivation**: These attackers carry out directives of a national government, targeting other countries' critical infrastructure, stealing intellectual property, or disrupting political processes (e.g., elections).
- **Methods**: Advanced persistent threats (APTs), espionage, and sabotage through digital means.
- **Profile**: These groups are highly sophisticated and well-funded, often with the backing of military or national intelligence agencies.

4. Insiders:

- **Motivation**: Insider threats can be motivated by personal grievances, financial gain, or coercion by external parties. Sometimes, their actions are unintentional, caused by negligence or lack of awareness.
- **Methods**: Data theft, sabotage, or misuse of access privileges.
- **Profile**: Insiders can be current or former employees, contractors, or business partners who have direct access to the organization's systems and data.

5. Script Kiddies:

- **Motivation**: Often driven by a desire for recognition among their peers, script kiddies are typically less skilled and do not develop their own hacking tools or methods.
- **Methods**: Use of readily available hacking tools and scripts to exploit known vulnerabilities.
- **Profile**: Usually, these are individuals with limited technical skills who are looking to make a quick impact without a concerted effort or sophisticated plan.

6. **White Hat Hackers:**
   - **Motivation**: Also known as ethical hackers, they help organizations identify security vulnerabilities to enhance their defensive strategies.
   - **Methods**: Penetration testing and security assessments conducted under authorization.
   - **Profile**: These can be individuals or companies specializing in cybersecurity services, often certified in their field.

2.3 Case Studies: Notable Cyber Attacks

This section explores several high-profile cyber attacks that have shaped the understanding of cybersecurity threats and their consequences. Each case study provides insights into the tactics used by attackers and the impact on the victims.

1. **WannaCry Ransomware Attack (2017):**
   - **Overview**: WannaCry was a widespread ransomware attack that targeted more than 200,000 computers spanning 150 countries. The malicious software encrypted data on compromised systems and demanded ransom payments in Bitcoin.
   - **Method**: The attack exploited a vulnerability in Microsoft Windows SMB protocol, which was leaked from the U.S. National Security Agency's stockpile of cyber weapons.
   - **Impact**: Major organizations affected included the UK's National Health Service (NHS), FedEx, and Spain's Telefónica. The attack caused disruptions in healthcare services, transport, and communications industries, with total damages estimated to be in the billions of dollars.

2. **Sony Pictures Hack (2014):**
   - **Overview**: Sony Pictures Entertainment experienced a severe cyber attack that resulted in the unauthorized disclosure of sensitive information, including personal emails, employee data, and unreleased movies.
   - **Method**: The attackers used a server message block (SMB) worm tool to gain access to Sony's network and deliver the destructive payload.
   - **Impact**: The attack resulted in the disclosure of sensitive personal and business information. It also led to significant financial losses and damaged the company's reputation. The U.S. government attributed the attack to North Korea, allegedly in retaliation for the movie "The Interview," which depicted a fictional assassination of its leader.

3. **Equifax Data Breach (2017):**
   - **Overview**: One of the most extensive data breaches to date, impacting about 147 million individuals, occurred with the exposure of personal information.
   - **Method**: The breach stemmed from exploiting a vulnerability within the Apache Struts web framework employed by Equifax's website.

- **Impact**: The compromised data included sensitive details like Social Security numbers, birth dates, addresses, and in certain instances, driver's license numbers. This breach sparked significant scrutiny concerning data protection protocols and led to a plethora of legal actions and regulatory measures against Equifax.

4. Stuxnet Worm (2010):

- **Overview**: Stuxnet, a remarkably advanced computer worm uncovered in 2010 but likely operational before 2009, aimed at industrial control systems within Iran's nuclear program.

- **Method:** The worm specifically focused on software and hardware produced by Siemens, which controlled centrifuges in nuclear facilities. It infiltrated the network through an infected USB flash drive, exploiting numerous zero-day vulnerabilities.

- **Impact:** Stuxnet effectively sabotaged around 1,000 centrifuges at Iran's Natanz uranium enrichment plant. This assault represented one of the initial instances of cyber weapons directed at physical infrastructure.

5. NotPetya Attack (2017):

- **Overview**: Originating in Ukraine, NotPetya was initially perceived as ransomware but later identified as a state-sponsored cyber weapon aimed at disruption.

- **Method**: It used the same vulnerabilities as WannaCry (the EternalBlue exploit) and additionally spread through a compromised Ukrainian accounting software update.

- **Impact**: NotPetya caused global disruption, particularly affecting multinational corporations with ties to Ukraine, including Maersk, Merck, and FedEx, with total damages estimated to be over $10 billion.

2.4 Threats to Personal vs. Corporate Security

Cyber threats impact both individuals and organizations, but the nature and implications of these threats can differ significantly based on the target. Understanding the distinct challenges faced by personal and corporate security can help in crafting more effective defense strategies.

Personal Security Threats

Personal cybersecurity focuses on protecting individuals from attacks that compromise their privacy, finances, and personal data. Common threats include:

- **Identity Theft**: Cybercriminals steal personal information to impersonate or commit fraud.
- **Phishing Attacks**: Individuals are targeted by emails or messages that aim to steal sensitive information like passwords and bank account details.
- **Malware**: Includes viruses and ransomware that can lead to data loss or financial demands.
- **Social Engineering**: Manipulative tactics employed to deceive individuals into committing security errors or divulging confidential information.

Impact on Individuals:

- **Financial Loss**: From drained bank accounts to credit card fraud.
- **Emotional Distress**: Identity theft and privacy breaches can cause significant stress and anxiety.
- **Reputation Damage**: Compromised social media accounts can be used to spread false information or offensive content.

Corporate Security Threats

Corporate or organizational cybersecurity focuses on protecting the assets and operations of an organization from attacks that could undermine its functionality and credibility. Common threats include:

- **Advanced Persistent Threats (APTs)**: Targeted attacks that linger undetected to steal data over a long period.
- **Data Breaches**: Unauthorized access to corporate data, which can be sensitive or proprietary.
- **Ransomware**: Targets corporate networks to encrypt critical data and demand ransom for its release.
- **Insider Threats**: Employees who intentionally or accidentally leak or compromise corporate data.

Impact on Organizations:

- **Operational Disruption**: Attacks can halt production lines, disable websites, or interrupt services.
- **Financial Loss**: Includes direct costs like ransom payments and indirect costs such as litigation, regulatory fines, and lost business.
- **Brand Damage**: A significant breach can erode customer trust and tarnish a company's reputation long-term.

Mitigation Strategies

For Personal Security:

- **Use of Strong Passwords**: Implementing strong, distinct passwords for each online account and activating two-factor authentication where possible.
- **Regular Software Updates**: Ensuring that operating systems, applications, and antivirus programs are regularly updated.
- **Education**: Familiarizing oneself with prevalent attacker strategies like phishing attacks and social engineering ploys.

For Corporate Security:

- **Comprehensive Security Framework**: Including policies, procedures, and technologies to protect network and data integrity.
- **Employee Training and Awareness Programs**: Regular training on security best practices and recognizing phishing attempts.
- **Incident Response and Business Continuity Plans**: Preparedness to respond to data breaches and ensure business operations can continue with minimal disruption.

2.5 The Global Impact of Cyber Threats

The influence of cyber threats extends far beyond individual or organizational disruption, affecting the global economy, international relations, and societal trust in digital technologies. As cyber threats have grown more sophisticated and pervasive, their global implications have become more significant and complex.

Economic Impact

Cyber threats pose a substantial economic burden globally. The costs associated with mitigating cyber attacks, recovering lost data, and repairing systems are immense. Additionally, significant financial resources are allocated to cybersecurity defenses, including investment in technologies, training, and compliance with evolving regulations.

- **Direct Costs**: This category encompasses direct costs incurred directly as a result of the attack, such as incident response measures, forensic examinations, and any ransom payments made, if applicable.
- **Indirect Costs**: Indirect costs that extend beyond the immediate aftermath of the attack, including harm to reputation, erosion of customer confidence, and potential legal ramifications stemming from breaches.

Impact on Critical Infrastructure

Cybersecurity risks targeting critical infrastructure, encompassing sectors like energy, transportation, and healthcare, present significant threats to both national security and public safety. A successful attack could lead to widespread service disruptions, endanger lives, and cause physical damage to facilities.

- **Utilities and Energy**: Disruptions can result in outages that affect everything from individual households to entire regions.

- **Healthcare**: Attacks can compromise hospital systems, leading to delays in medical procedures and risks to patient safety.

Political and Geopolitical Consequences

Cyber threats are increasingly used as instruments in geopolitical conflicts, with nations employing cyber capabilities to influence elections, steal sensitive government data, and disrupt the political stability of adversaries.

- **Election Security**: Cyber attacks aimed at election infrastructure can undermine public confidence in electoral processes and democratic governance.
- **Espionage**: State-sponsored cyber espionage involves the theft of critical national security information or intellectual property to bolster a country's economic, technological, or military advantage.

Social Implications

The prevalence of cyber threats contributes to an atmosphere of mistrust towards digital technologies and platforms. Concerns about privacy breaches and data misuse can inhibit users' engagement with online services, impacting digital commerce, social interactions, and access to information.

- **Privacy Concerns**: Frequent data breaches have heightened public concern over personal data privacy and security.
- **Trust in Digital Systems**: There's a growing hesitance to trust institutions that fail to protect sensitive information, affecting user behavior and technology adoption rates.

Global Response and Cooperation

Addressing the global nature of cyber threats requires international cooperation and coordinated efforts among nations. This includes sharing intelligence about threats, harmonizing legal frameworks to prosecute cybercrimes, and setting global standards for cybersecurity practices.

- **International Cybersecurity Alliances**: Organizations like INTERPOL and various UN initiatives facilitate collaboration on cybersecurity threats and responses.
- **Regulatory Efforts**: Laws and regulations such as the GDPR in the EU and other national laws aim to protect data and ensure companies maintain high security standards.

Chapter 3: Fundamental Cybersecurity Concepts

3.1 The CIA Triad: Confidentiality, Integrity, Availability

The CIA Triad stands as a prevalent framework, offering guidance for information security policies within organizational settings. The three components of the CIA Triad—Confidentiality, Integrity, and Availability—are the pillars upon which the security of any information system is built. Understanding and implementing these three elements effectively can significantly enhance an organization's security posture.

Confidentiality

Confidentiality involves ensuring that information is accessible only to those authorized to have access. It is about protecting personal or proprietary information from unauthorized individuals or systems. This is crucial for maintaining the privacy of sensitive data, such as financial records, personal data, and intellectual property.

- **Techniques to Ensure Confidentiality**:
  - **Encryption**: Transforming readable data into an unreadable format unless decrypted by authorized parties.
  - **Access Controls**: Limiting access to data through authentication and authorization mechanisms.
  - **Data Classification**: Classifying data based on its level of sensitivity to enforce appropriate security controls.

Integrity

Integrity refers to maintaining the accuracy and completeness of data. It ensures that information is trustworthy and not altered in transit or after storage by unauthorized or unauthorized means. Integrity is critical for operational and decision-making processes within any business or organization.

- **Techniques to Ensure Integrity**:
  - **Hash Functions**: Using algorithms to generate a unique value from a data item to detect changes and verify data integrity.
  - **Digital Signatures**: Providing a means to verify the authenticity of a digital message or document.
  - **Audit Trails**: Keeping detailed logs that track who accessed information and what changes were made can help in detecting and tracing unauthorized modifications.

Availability

Availability ensures that information is accessible to authorized users when needed. Maintaining availability is vital for operational success, as disruptions can lead to lost productivity, revenue, and even harm the user's trust.

- **Techniques to Ensure Availability**:
  - **Redundancy**: Building additional capacity that can be called upon in the event of system failure.

- **Failover Systems**: Creating systems that can seamlessly take over if the primary system fails.
- **Regular Maintenance**: Conducting hardware repairs, software updates, and addressing vulnerabilities promptly to prevent downtime.

Balancing the CIA Triad

It's important to understand that the elements of the CIA Triad are interrelated and that a balance must be struck between them according to the organization's needs and resources. Overemphasizing one element can lead to weaknesses in another. For instance, overly stringent access controls (enhancing confidentiality) might impede the availability of data to authorized users when they need it most.

Application in Cybersecurity Strategies:

The CIA Triad should be at the heart of any organization's cybersecurity strategy. By assessing the threats against each element of the triad, organizations can allocate resources and apply controls effectively to mitigate risks. This strategic approach not only protects information but also supports the organization's objectives and regulatory compliance efforts.

Understanding the CIA Triad provides a clear framework for discussing and evaluating cybersecurity policies and actions. It helps in pinpointing vulnerabilities in the information systems and devising comprehensive measures to protect against cyber threats, ensuring the security and resilience of organizational operations.

3.2 Basics of Cryptography

Cryptography serves as a cornerstone in cybersecurity, safeguarding information by ensuring its confidentiality, integrity, and authenticity. It employs mathematical principles and computational algorithms to transform data into a secure format, accessible only to authorized recipients. A fundamental grasp of cryptography is imperative for all individuals involved in securing information systems.

Cryptography Overview

Cryptography entails the creation of codes to keep information hidden, employing encryption and decryption technologies to secure communications. This ensures that data transmitted across networks remains trustworthy and impervious to adversaries.

Key Concepts

1. Encryption: The process of converting plaintext with an encryption key and an algorithm into ciphertext.
2. Decryption: The process of reversing encryption, where a decryption key is used to transform ciphertext back into plaintext.
3. Cipher: An algorithm for encryption or decryption, defining a precise set of steps.

Types of Cryptography

1. Symmetric-Key Cryptography:
   - Utilizes a single key shared between sender and receiver for encryption and decryption.

- Key secrecy is paramount to maintain message security.

2. Asymmetric-Key Cryptography:

    - Employs distinct public and private keys, with the public key distributed openly and the private key kept secret.
    - Facilitates secure data transmission, digital signatures, and key exchange.

3. Hash Functions:

    - Generates a fixed-size string of bytes (hash) from an input, ensuring data integrity by detecting even minor alterations in the message.

Applications

- Data Security: Encrypting stored or cloud-based data prevents unauthorized access.
- Secure Communication: Encrypting data during transmission, including emails, instant messaging, and VoIP calls.
- Authentication: Verifying user identities and message origins using cryptographic techniques like digital signatures.
- Non-repudiation: Ensuring message senders cannot deny transmission, typically achieved through digital signatures.

Challenges

- Key Management: Secure storage and handling of cryptographic keys are vital for maintaining security.
- Computational Cost: Encryption and decryption can strain computational resources, impacting system performance.
- Quantum Computing: The emergence of quantum computers poses a potential threat to current cryptographic algorithms, prompting research into quantum-resistant cryptography.

3.3 Authentication Methods

Before allowing access to resources in an information system, users, systems, or other entities must authenticate themselves. Effective authentication methods help ensure that users are who they claim to be and prevent unauthorized access, thereby protecting sensitive data and systems from potential breaches.

Overview of Authentication

Authentication is typically the first step in an access control process, serving as the gatekeeper for systems and data. It involves validating credentials against stored records of user information, which can include passwords, digital certificates, or biometric data.

Types of Authentication Factors

Authentication methods are often categorized by the type of evidence they require from the user. These are known as "factors" of authentication:

1. **Something You Know (Knowledge Factor):**

    - **Passwords and PINs:** The most common authentication method, which involves a secret word or series of characters only known to the user.

    - **Security Questions:** Personal questions (e.g., mother's maiden name, first pet's name) used as a secondary form of authentication.

2. **Something You Have (Possession Factor):**

    - **Security Tokens:** Hardware needed to access a resource that is limited electronically. This can be a USB token, a smart card, or a mobile app that generates time-based, one-time passwords (TOTPs).

    - **Software Tokens:** Software-based security tokens are installed on devices and can generate a code for two-factor authentication.

3. **Something You Are (Inherence Factor):**

    - **Biometrics:** This covers iris scans, voice recognition, facial recognition, and fingerprints. Biometrics are unique to the individual and are difficult to forge or steal.

Advanced Authentication Methods

- **Multi-Factor Authentication (MFA):**

    - Integrates two or more independent credentials: knowledge-based, possession-based, or biometric, to verify the user's identity.

    - MFA offers enhanced security compared to single-factor methods by requiring multiple forms of verification.

- **Single Sign-On (SSO):**

    - Integrates two or more independent credentials: knowledge-based, possession-based, or biometric, to verify the user's identity.

- MFA offers enhanced security compared to single-factor methods by requiring multiple forms of verification.
- **Certificate-Based Authentication:**
  - Relies on digital certificates, electronic documents utilized to validate ownership of a public key.

Challenges and Considerations

- **Password Management:** Despite their ubiquity, passwords are vulnerable to theft and require strong policies and management tools to remain effective.
- **Biometric Security:** While biometrics offer strong security, they also raise privacy concerns and are not infallible.
- **Implementation Costs:** Some advanced authentication methods, like biometrics or smart cards, require substantial investment in terms of hardware and software infrastructure.

3.4 Secure Communication Protocols

Secure communication protocols are vital for safeguarding data as it traverses networks, ensuring confidentiality, integrity, and authentication. These protocols form the backbone of secure data exchanges across various domains, including personal communications, business transactions, and governmental operations.

Overview of Secure Communication Protocols

A communication protocol establishes rules for transmitting information between entities in a communications system. Secure communication protocols are specifically designed to protect transmitted data through encryption, authentication, integrity checks, and other security measures.

Key Secure Communication Protocols

1. **Hypertext Transfer Protocol Secure (HTTPS):**
   - HTTPS extends HTTP for secure communication over computer networks, widely used on the Internet.
   - Uses Secure Sockets Layer (SSL) or Transport Layer Security (TLS) to authenticate and encrypt communication.

2. **Secure Sockets Layer (SSL)/Transport Layer Security (TLS):**
   - SSL and TLS are cryptographic protocols securing communications over computer networks.
   - Encrypts data transmission and provides authentication of communicating parties.

3. **Secure Shell (SSH):**
   - SSH ensures secure operation of network services over unsecured networks, facilitating remote command-line login and execution.
   - Establishes secure channels between client and server applications.

4. **IPsec (Internet Protocol Security):**
   - The Internet Protocol (IP) security suite encrypts and authenticates every IP packet to safeguard IP connections.
   - Includes protocols for mutual authentication and cryptographic key negotiation.

5. **Pretty Good Privacy (PGP)/GNU Privacy Guard (GPG):**
   - PGP and GPG encrypt and decrypt data, providing cryptographic privacy and authentication.
   - Commonly used for securing emails, ensuring confidentiality and authenticating senders.

Challenges and Considerations

- **Implementation Complexity:** Proper implementation of secure communication protocols demands technical expertise.
- **Performance Overhead:** Encryption and decryption processes can strain computational resources, impacting system performance.
- **Interoperability:** Ensuring compatibility among different systems and devices using secure protocols requires meticulous configuration and management.

3.5 The Role of Anonymity and Privacy

Anonymity and privacy are pivotal aspects of cybersecurity, intricately connected yet distinct in their objectives and implications. In the digital realm, privacy entails managing one's personal information, controlling its sharing and accessibility. Conversely, anonymity involves being unidentifiable within a given context, even if certain aspects of one's identity are discernible. Together, these concepts play a crucial role in shielding individuals and organizations from unwarranted surveillance, identity theft, and other malicious activities.

Importance of Anonymity and Privacy

1. **Protecting Personal Information:** Anonymity shields individuals from targeted attacks by concealing their true identity, while privacy empowers them to regulate access to personal data.
2. **Freedom of Expression:** Anonymity enables individuals to express themselves without fear of reprisal, especially in politically restrictive environments.
3. **Avoiding Targeted Advertising:** Privacy safeguards help individuals evade intrusive and exploitative targeted advertisements tailored to their personal habits and preferences.
4. **Preventing Identity Theft:** Privacy measures mitigate the risk of identity theft, which can inflict severe financial and personal harm.

Challenges to Anonymity and Privacy

- **Advanced Tracking Techniques:** Technologies such as fingerprinting and facial recognition undermine anonymity, while data aggregation practices pose substantial privacy risks.

- **Legal and Regulatory Hurdles:** Privacy protections vary across jurisdictions, posing compliance challenges for global entities.
- **Social Engineering Attacks:** Malicious actors exploit personal information for nefarious purposes, underscoring the need for robust privacy safeguards.

Technological Tools for Anonymity and Privacy

1. **Encryption:** Crucial for data privacy, encryption ensures that only authorized parties can access data, whether stored or transmitted.

2. **Virtual Private Networks (VPNs):** VPNs establish secure and private networks over public internet connections, concealing users' IP addresses and online activities.

3. **Anonymous Browsers:** Tools like the Tor browser enable anonymous web browsing by routing internet traffic through multiple servers, obscuring users' locations and activities.

4. **Privacy-Enhancing Technologies (PETs):** These technologies, such as differential privacy and zero-knowledge proofs, minimize personal data use while preserving data utility.

Implementing Privacy and Anonymity Measures

- **Data Minimization:** Collect only essential data to reduce exposure and deter hackers.
- **Regular Audits:** Perform routine privacy audits to verify compliance and pinpoint any weaknesses in data management practices.
- **Awareness and Training:** Provide comprehensive education and training sessions to staff and users, emphasizing the significance of privacy and imparting knowledge on identifying and thwarting social engineering attacks.

Chapter 4: Cybersecurity Best Practices

4.1 Creating Strong Passwords

Strong passwords considerably lower the risk of breaches and cyberattacks by acting as the main line of defense against unwanted access to online accounts and personal data. Below are best practices for generating strong passwords and strategies for maintaining their security over time.

Characteristics of Strong Passwords

1. **Length:** Opt for passwords that are at least 12-16 characters long, as longer passwords offer greater security due to the increased number of combinations.

2. **Complexity:** Include a mix of uppercase letters, lowercase letters, numbers, and special characters to thwart brute force and dictionary attacks.

3. **Unpredictability:** Avoid common words, phrases, or easily guessed patterns, such as sequential keyboard paths or repeated characters.

Creating Strong Passwords

- **Use a Passphrase:** Create a random passphrase consisting of unrelated words and characters, such as "Blue#Fish@Market!29".

- **Incorporate Personalization Tricks:** Customize passphrases using personal tricks to enhance memorability while maintaining security.

- **Steer Clear of Personal Information:** Don't use information that can be easily accessed, such as family member names, birthdays, or pet names.

Password Management Best Practices

- **Use a Password Manager:** To ensure strong and unique passwords for numerous accounts, utilize a password manager to create, store, and retrieve complicated passwords.

- **Change Passwords Regularly:** Update passwords periodically and whenever there's suspicion of compromise, although opinions on frequency may vary.

- **Enable Multi-Factor Authentication (MFA):** Add an extra layer of security by requiring more than just a password for account access.

Educating Users on Password Security

- **Regular Training:** Conduct training sessions to educate users on password security importance and effective password creation and management.

- **Security Policies:** Implement organizational security policies mandating the use of strong passwords and regular password updates.

Avoid Common Mistakes

- **Password Reuse**: To reduce the dangers associated with a single hack, avoid using the same password on several different websites.
- **Writing Down Passwords:** Avoid storing passwords in unsecured locations, opting instead for secure storage methods accessible only to you.

Strong passwords are integral to securing personal and organizational data. Adhering to these guidelines significantly bolsters online security posture. But keep in mind that creating secure passwords is only one part of an all-encompassing cybersecurity plan. Combining them with other security practices like regular software updates and enabling MFA ensures robust defense against cyber threats.

4.2 Regular Updates and Patch Management

Regular updates and patch management are fundamental pillars of a comprehensive cybersecurity strategy, encompassing the systematic review, acquisition, testing, and installation of software updates, patches, and improvements provided by vendors. These practices are vital for correcting security vulnerabilities, enhancing functionality, and ensuring the overall health and security of technology environments.

Importance of Regular Updates and Patch Management

1. **Security:** Cyber attacks often exploit known vulnerabilities in software. Regular updates and patching help mitigate these risks by closing vulnerabilities and reducing the likelihood of data breaches and attacks.
2. **Performance:** Updates not only address security flaws but also enhance stability, performance, and usability of software and systems.
3. **Compliance:** Many industries mandate regular updates and patch management as compliance requirements. Non-compliance can lead to penalties and increased legal risks.

Challenges in Patch Management

- **Asset Tracking:** Maintaining an inventory of all IT assets can be challenging, leading to some systems being overlooked during patching.
- **Patch Prioritization:** Not all patches are equally critical. Prioritization should be based on severity and relevance to the environment.
- **Testing:** Patches need thorough testing to ensure they don't cause issues with existing systems, which can be time-consuming.

Best Practices for Effective Patch Management

1. **Develop a Patch Management Policy:** Establish clear policies defining patch management procedures, including schedules, responsibilities, testing, and prioritization criteria.
2. **Automate Patch Management:** Utilize tools to automate patch discovery, deployment, and verification, reducing workload and minimizing human error.
3. **Maintain Asset Inventory:** Keep an up-to-date inventory of all IT assets to ensure no device is overlooked during patching.

4. **Regular Review and Testing:** Test patches in a controlled environment before deployment to prevent interference with existing systems or introduction of vulnerabilities.

5. **Educate and Train Staff:** Ensure IT staff understand patch management importance and procedures, and educate non-IT staff on applying updates to their devices.

Patch Management Tools

Specialized patch management software streamlines the process by detecting patch status, prioritizing patches, and automating deployment. Examples include Microsoft SCCM, IBM BigFix, and VMware vCenter Configuration Manager.

4.3 Principles of Least Privilege

A fundamental idea in cybersecurity is the principle of least privilege (PoLP), which suggests that people and systems should only have the minimal amount of access necessary for their operations. This approach mitigates potential damage arising from accidents, errors, or malicious activities. Implementing PoLP is indispensable for safeguarding sensitive information and systems while upholding a secure and efficient IT environment.

Understanding the Principle of Least Privilege

- **Definition:** PoLP dictates that all users, processes, and systems should operate with the least amount of privilege required to fulfill their tasks.

- **Purpose:** By limiting access rights, PoLP mitigates the risk of inadvertent or deliberate misuse of authority, which could result in data breaches or system disruptions.

Application of the Principle of Least Privilege

1. **User Accounts:** Standard users should not possess administrative rights, and broader network access should be granted only as necessary. Administrative privileges should be utilized sparingly.

2. **Applications and Systems:** Applications and system processes should function with minimal privileges to mitigate risks associated with potential vulnerabilities being exploited by attackers.

3. **Network Access:** Access to network segments should be restricted, ensuring that devices and users can only connect to resources essential for their tasks.

Implementing Least Privilege

1. **Role-Based Access Control (RBAC):** Employ access controls based on organizational roles, granting users permissions pertinent to their responsibilities.

2. **Regular Audits of Access Rights:** Conduct periodic reviews to ensure appropriate user privileges and prevent unnecessary access.

3. **Privileged Access Management (PAM) Tools:** Utilize tools to manage and monitor privileged accounts, ensuring their judicious use.

4. **Separation of Duties:** Divide critical functions among multiple individuals to thwart fraud and unauthorized access.

5. **Just-in-Time (JIT) Privileges:** Adopt JIT provisioning of privileges, granting access only for the duration required to complete specific tasks.

Benefits of Least Privilege

- **Reduced Attack Surface:** Limiting privileges reduces potential entry points for attackers, diminishing the risk of security breaches.

- **Lower Risk of Internal Threats:** By restricting access, PoLP mitigates damage from insider threats, whether malicious or accidental.

- **Compliance:** PoLP aids compliance with regulatory requirements mandating stringent controls over sensitive data access.

Challenges in Implementing Least Privilege

- **Complexity in Large Organizations:** Enforcing access controls in large organizations, especially amidst role and responsibility changes, can be intricate.

- **User Resistance:** Users accustomed to broad access may resist privilege restrictions, perceiving them as impediments to efficiency.

- **Finding a Balance Between Security and Usability**: One of the most typical challenges is balancing resource security with user productivity.

4.4 Safe Internet Browsing Habits

Safe internet browsing habits are paramount for safeguarding individuals and organizations against online threats. Despite its immense utility, the internet also harbors significant security risks. Cultivating and maintaining good browsing habits can substantially diminish the likelihood of encountering malware, phishing attempts, and other cyber threats.

Key Safe Browsing Practices

1. **Use Secure Connections:** Prioritize websites with HTTPS, particularly when divulging sensitive information like credit card details or passwords.

2. **Keep Browser and Plugins Updated:** Regularly update your web browser and plugins to shield against security vulnerabilities.

3. **Use Caution When Downloading:** Avoid clicking on pop-up advertisements or downloading files from unreliable sites, as these actions are frequently used as vectors for the spread of malware.

4. **Utilize Strong, Unique Passwords:** Employ strong, unique passwords for all online accounts, and consider employing a password manager for enhanced security.

5. **Enable Multi-Factor Authentication (MFA):** Fortify account security with MFA, requiring an additional verification step alongside passwords.

6. **Identify and Evade Phishing Attempts:** Exercise caution with emails or messages requesting personal information and verify their authenticity through official channels.

7. **Leverage Privacy-Enhancing Tools:** Employ browser extensions such as ad blockers, script blockers, or anti-tracking tools to bolster privacy.

8. **Exercise Caution with Public Wi-Fi:** Refrain from conducting sensitive transactions over public Wi-Fi networks and utilize VPNs for enhanced security.

Implementing Safe Browsing Policies in Organizations

- **Educational Programs:** Regularly educate employees on safe browsing practices and emerging online threats through training sessions.

- **Enforce Security Policies:** Enact organizational policies that promote safe browsing, including restrictions on accessing potentially hazardous websites and mandatory VPN usage for remote access.

- **Monitor and Control Internet Use:** Make use of technologies to keep an eye on how the company uses the internet, preventing access to unlicensed apps and dangerous websites.

- **Regular Security Audits:** Conduct periodic security audits to assess the efficacy of existing browsing policies and practices, identifying and rectifying any security gaps.

4.5 Physical Security Measures

Physical security measures are often sidelined in cybersecurity discussions, yet they are pivotal in shielding an organization's digital assets. These measures thwart unauthorized physical access to critical infrastructure, hardware, and data storage areas, acting as a deterrent against theft, vandalism, and espionage.

Importance of Physical Security in Cybersecurity

Physical breaches can inflict as much damage as cyber attacks, if not more. Unauthorized entry into server rooms or data centers can bypass even the most robust cybersecurity defenses, granting direct access to sensitive information.

Key Physical Security Measures

1. **Access Control Systems:** Employ systems like key card access, biometric scanners, or PIN pads to restrict entry to sensitive areas.
2. **Surveillance Systems:** Utilize CCTV cameras to monitor premises round-the-clock, particularly critical entry points and sensitive areas.
3. **Security Personnel:** Deploy trained security personnel to monitor key access points and respond swiftly to security breaches.
4. **Secure Workstations and Devices:** Physically secure workstations with cable locks and implement a clean desk policy for sensitive information.
5. **Data Destruction Protocols:** Establish secure disposal policies for sensitive information, including shredding paper documents and wiping electronic data.
6. **Visitor Management:** Enforce strict visitor management policies, logging visitors in and out and issuing visitor badges.
7. **Environmental Controls:** Safeguard critical infrastructure from environmental threats with appropriate detection and suppression systems.
8. **Device Management:** Maintain an inventory of hardware devices and promptly address lost or stolen devices.

Challenges in Implementing Physical Security

- **Cost:** Comprehensive physical security measures can be costly, especially for larger organizations.
- **Complacency:** Employees may grow complacent about physical security, leading to lapses in protocol adherence.
- **Balancing Access and Security**: It might be difficult to strike a balance between protecting resources and preserving output.

Chapter 5: Secure Your Devices and Networks

5.1 Home Network Security Basics

Home networks are increasingly targeted by cyber attackers due to the rise in connected devices and often lax security measures compared to corporate networks. Securing your home network is vital to safeguard personal information, prevent unauthorized access to devices, and ensure online safety. Here are fundamental steps and best practices for securing a home network:

Understanding Home Network Security

Protecting a home network involves safeguarding the network connecting personal computing devices to each other and the internet. It defends against intrusions, malware, and cyber threats that could compromise personal data.

Essential Steps to Secure Your Home Network

1. **Change Default Router Settings:** Customize admin credentials, network name (SSID), and Wi-Fi password to prevent unauthorized access.
2. **Enable Strong Encryption:** Use WPA3 or WPA2 encryption for Wi-Fi networks to enhance security.
3. **Update Router Firmware:** Install firmware updates regularly to patch security vulnerabilities and improve performance.
4. **Disable Unused Features:** Turn off features like Remote Management, UPnP, and WPS if not in use to reduce attack surface.
5. **Use a Firewall:** Activate the router's built-in firewall and enable firewalls on all connected devices.
6. **Create a Guest Network:** Set up a separate Wi-Fi network for guests to isolate personal devices from potential threats.
7. **Secure IoT Devices:** Change default passwords and update software on all smart home devices regularly.
8. **Regular Network Monitoring:** Monitor connected devices and access logs for unusual activity or unauthorized access.

Best Practices for Network Management

- **Educate Household Members:** Teach everyone in the household about network security and safe internet usage practices.
- **Use VPNs for Privacy:** Employ a VPN for enhanced privacy, especially when accessing sensitive information.
- **Backup Important Data:** Regularly back up data from connected devices to separate storage solutions for recovery in case of data loss.

Protecting a home network demands continual attention, upkeep, and proactive application of security protocols. Adhering to these procedures can substantially enhance your home network's security and safeguard personal devices against cyber threats.

5.2 Securing Personal Computers and Laptops

Securing personal computers and laptops is crucial for safeguarding sensitive information and preventing cyber threats. Here are key strategies to effectively safeguard these devices:

Understanding the Importance of Device Security

Personal computers and laptops store personal data, access online services, and connect to various networks, making them vulnerable to cyber threats.

Essential Security Measures for Computers and Laptops

1. **Install Antivirus and Anti-Malware Software:** Use reputable antivirus software and keep it updated to protect against malware threats.
2. **Keep Operating Systems and Software Updated:** Regularly install updates for the operating system and installed software to patch security vulnerabilities.
3. **Enable Firewall Protection:** Ensure the device's firewall is enabled to block unauthorized access while permitting outward communication.
4. **Use Strong Passwords and Authentication:** Protect the device with a strong, unique password and consider enabling multi-factor authentication (MFA) for added security.
5. **Encrypt Sensitive Data:** Use encryption tools to protect sensitive data stored on the device, ensuring it is unreadable to unauthorized users.
6. **Secure Wi-Fi Connections:** Connect to secure, trusted Wi-Fi networks, and use a VPN in public places to encrypt internet connections.
7. **Practice Safe Browsing and Email Habits:** Be cautious about clicking links or opening attachments in emails to prevent phishing attacks.
8. **Backup Important Data Regularly:** Back up important files to external drives or cloud storage to prevent data loss in the event of hardware failure or ransomware attacks.
9. **Physical Security Measures:** Secure laptops with cable locks when not in use, especially in public areas, and use privacy screens to prevent "shoulder surfing."
10. **Disable Auto-Run Features:** Disable auto-run settings to prevent automatic execution of files from connected devices like USB drives.

Best Practices for Device Management

- **User Account Management:** Use non-administrator accounts for daily activities and reserve administrator accounts for system changes and installations.
- **Regular Security Audits:** Perform regular security checks and audits to ensure security measures are up to date and effective.
- **Educate Yourself and Others:** Stay informed about cybersecurity threats and educate family members or other users about the importance of security.

Securing personal computers and laptops requires technical measures, user education, and regular maintenance. By implementing these strategies, you can enhance the security of your devices and protect your digital information.

5.3 Protecting Mobile Devices: Phones and Tablets

Securing mobile devices is essential for protecting personal and professional information from cyber threats. Here are key strategies to safeguard mobile devices and sensitive data:

Understanding Mobile Device Security

Mobile devices store personal and professional information and are frequently used to access corporate networks, making their security crucial for data integrity.

Essential Security Measures for Mobile Devices

1. **Install Updates Promptly:** Regularly update the device's operating system and apps to patch known vulnerabilities.
2. **Use Strong Authentication:** Implement strong passwords, PINs, or biometric authentication to lock devices.
3. **Install Reputable Security Apps:** Use trusted antivirus and security apps to protect against malware and unauthorized access.
4. **Enable Remote Wiping and Location Tracking:** Activate features to remotely locate, lock, or wipe the device if lost or stolen.
5. **Secure Network Connections:** Avoid unsecured public Wi-Fi networks and use a VPN for encryption on public networks.
6. **Beware of App Permissions:** Download apps from reputable sources and review app permissions to prevent unnecessary data access.
7. **Disable Bluetooth and NFC When Not in Use:** Turn off Bluetooth and NFC to prevent unauthorized connections.
8. **Use Encryption:** Enable encryption settings to protect stored data even if the device is compromised.
9. **Beware of Phishing Attacks:** Be cautious about opening links or downloading attachments from unknown sources.
10. **Backup Data Regularly:** Backup data to secure locations to prevent data loss due to device failure or theft.

Best Practices for Device Management

- **Educate Yourself and Others:** Stay informed about mobile security threats and educate family or colleagues on best practices.
- **Physical Security:** Keep devices secure and within sight to prevent physical theft.

- **Regular Security Audits:** Conduct audits to ensure security measures are up-to-date and effective, including reviewing installed apps.

5.4 Securing IoT Devices in the Smart Home

Securing IoT devices is crucial to prevent them from becoming entry points for cyberattacks. Here are essential security measures:

Understanding IoT Device Security

IoT devices connect to the internet and each other, enhancing home automation but introducing vulnerabilities due to their connectivity.

Essential Security Measures for IoT Devices

1. **Change Default Settings:** Immediately change default usernames and passwords to unique and strong ones.
2. **Regularly Update Firmware:** Ensure devices are set to automatically update or manually check for updates to patch security vulnerabilities.
3. **Secure Your Network:** Place IoT devices on a separate network from main computing devices and use features like guest networks on routers.
4. **Disable Unnecessary Features:** Turn off unused features and services to reduce potential attack surfaces.
5. **Use Strong Encryption:** Confirm encryption practices for data sent by IoT devices, especially involving personal data.
6. **Monitor Connected Devices:** Keep an inventory of devices and monitor for suspicious activity using security systems or routers.
7. **Implement Secure Authentication:** Use multi-factor authentication (MFA) for remote control interfaces if supported.
8. **Physical Security:** Ensure physical security of devices, especially those outdoors, to prevent tampering and theft.
9. **Educate All Users:** Ensure everyone understands the importance of IoT device security, including basic practices like not sharing passwords and recognizing phishing attempts.

Challenges in IoT Security

- **Diverse Ecosystem:** Devices come from different manufacturers with varying security standards, making uniform security protocols challenging.
- **Lack of Updates:** Some devices may rarely receive firmware updates, or manufacturers may stop providing updates.
- **Complexity in Management:** Managing security across numerous devices in smart homes can be challenging.

5.5 Using Public and Private Wi-Fi Safely

Understanding how to safely use both public and private Wi-Fi networks is crucial in protecting your data from potential security risks. Here are some best practices:

Understanding Wi-Fi Security Risks

Public Wi-Fi networks, in particular, pose higher risks due to minimal security measures, making them prime targets for cybercriminals to intercept data or spread malware.

Best Practices for Using Private Wi-Fi Safely

1. **Secure Your Wireless Router:**
   - Change default router settings, update firmware, and use strong encryption like WPA3 or WPA2.

2. **Disable Remote Management:**
   - Turn off remote management features to prevent external access to router settings.

3. **Use a Strong Wi-Fi Password:**
   - Create a unique, strong password for your Wi-Fi network to prevent unauthorized access.

4. **Enable Network Encryption:**
   - Encrypt your Wi-Fi network to protect transmitted data.

5. **Limit Network Access:**
   - Use MAC address filtering to allow only recognized devices to connect.

Best Practices for Using Public Wi-Fi Safely

1. **Use a VPN:**
   - Encrypt your internet traffic to protect data from eavesdroppers even on public Wi-Fi.

2. **Avoid Accessing Sensitive Information:**
   - Refrain from sensitive transactions unless necessary, and use a secure VPN connection.

3. **Turn Off Sharing:**
   - Disable file sharing and other sharing settings on your device.

4. **Use Secure Websites:**
   - Ensure websites use HTTPS to encrypt data transmission.

5. **Forget the Network After Use:**
   - Prevent automatic connection to public Wi-Fi networks after use to avoid data exposure.

6. **Keep Your Firewall Enabled:**
   - Activate your device's firewall to block malicious traffic.

7. **Monitor for SSL Certificates:**
    - Be cautious of certificate warnings indicating potential man-in-the-middle attacks.

Challenges in Wi-Fi Security

- Overconfidence in Security Measures
- Complexity in VPN Use
- Variability in Public Wi-Fi Security

Chapter 6: The Role of Antivirus and Firewalls

6.1 How Antivirus Software Works

Antivirus software is vital for cybersecurity defense, providing protection against malware and other cyber threats. Understanding its functions and challenges can help users and organizations make informed decisions about selecting and managing antivirus solutions.

Overview of Antivirus Software

Antivirus software detects, prevents, and removes malware from computers, networks, and storage devices. It continuously monitors activities and scans for known threats to maintain system integrity and security.

Core Functions of Antivirus Software

1. **Real-Time Scanning:**

    - Antivirus software monitors activities and scans files as they are opened, executed, or saved to detect malware in real-time.

2. **Virus Definition Database:**

    - Antivirus programs use virus definitions or signatures to recognize known malware. Regular updates of these definitions are essential to detect new threats.

3. **Heuristic Analysis:**

    - Modern antivirus software employs heuristic analysis to identify unknown viruses or variants by examining program behaviors for suspicious activity.

4. **System Scanning:**

    - Scheduled and manual scans check all files or specific directories for malware to ensure comprehensive protection.

5. **Quarantine and Removal:**

    - Detected threats are moved to a quarantine zone to isolate them from the system, allowing users to decide whether to delete or restore them.

6. **Reporting and Logging:**

    - Antivirus programs provide reports and logs of detected threats and actions taken, offering insights into security threats and antivirus effectiveness.

Types of Malware Detected by Antivirus Software

- **Viruses and Worms:** Self-replicating programs that damage systems and spread to other computers.
- **Trojans:** Malicious programs disguised as legitimate software.
- **Ransomware:** Malicious software that encrypts data and demands payment in exchange for decryption.

- **Adware and Spyware:** Software that tracks activities and gathers information without consent.
- **Rootkits:** Tools used to gain unauthorized access to a computer and mask intrusion.

Challenges in Antivirus Software

- **Zero-Day Exploits:** New malware variants can evade detection until a signature is available.
- **Performance Impact:** Antivirus software may slow down systems, especially during full scans.
- **False Positives:** Legitimate programs may be incorrectly identified as malware, causing disruptions.

6.2 Choosing the Right Antivirus

Selecting the right antivirus software is crucial for effective protection against malware and other cyber threats. With numerous options available, considering several factors ensures the chosen antivirus meets your specific security needs, whether for personal or organizational use.

Key Considerations When Choosing Antivirus Software:

1. **Detection Rate:**
   - Choose antivirus software with high detection rates, often reported in independent lab tests by organizations like AV-TEST and AV-Comparatives.

2. **System Impact:**
   - Assess resource usage, considering system memory and CPU usage. Effective protection shouldn't significantly slow down your computer.

3. **Features:**
   - Determine what features you need, such as a firewall, email scanning, anti-phishing, parental controls, and multi-device protection.

4. **Ease of Use:**
   - Opt for an intuitive user interface with straightforward navigation and scheduling options.

5. **Support and Customer Service:**
   - Ensure the provider offers reliable customer support through multiple channels like live chat, email, and phone.

6. **Price:**
   - Balance your budget with the need for advanced features and improved security offered by paid versions.

7. **Reputation:**
   - Research the reputation of the antivirus manufacturer through user reviews and professional evaluations.

8. **Compatibility:**
    - Confirm compatibility with your operating system and existing applications.

9. **Update Frequency:**
    - Choose software that updates its malware database frequently to provide protection against the latest threats.

Additional Factors for Businesses:

- **Scalability:** Ensure the antivirus solution can scale with business growth without performance degradation.

- **Central Management:** Look for solutions that offer centralized management for deploying updates, managing policies, and monitoring threats across multiple devices.

- **Compliance:** Verify compliance with industry regulations and standards, especially for businesses handling sensitive data.

6.3 The Importance of Firewalls

Firewalls serve as essential components of network security, acting as protective barriers between trusted internal networks and potentially harmful external networks like the internet. They monitor and control incoming and outgoing network traffic based on predefined security rules, effectively functioning as gatekeepers to determine which traffic should be allowed and which should be blocked.

Understanding Firewalls:

A firewall is a network security device that operates at various levels of the OSI model, depending on its type. It filters traffic and prevents unauthorized access to or from private networks, helping to safeguard sensitive data and systems from cyber threats. Different types of firewalls include:

- **Packet Filtering Firewalls:** These quickly inspect unencrypted packets and make decisions based on criteria such as IP addresses, port numbers, and protocols.

- **Stateful Inspection Firewalls:** They take context and state into account, offering more granular control by tracking active connections.

- **Proxy Firewalls:** These filter network traffic at the application level, acting as intermediaries between end-users and the web pages they access, allowing for deep content inspection.

- **Next-Generation Firewalls (NGFW):** These combine conventional firewall technology with supplementary features such as encrypted traffic analysis, intrusion prevention systems, and sophisticated application-level scrutiny.

Why Firewalls Matter:

Firewalls provide several critical security functions that help maintain network integrity and security:

- **Enhanced Security:** They serve as the first line of defense against unauthorized access to networks and computers.

- **Virus and Malware Prevention:** Properly configured firewalls can prevent many types of malware and viruses from entering a network.
- **Controlled Access:** Firewalls enforce security policies by controlling traffic based on rules set by the network administrator.
- **Traffic Monitoring:** They monitor and log traffic, aiding in the detection and response to suspicious activity.
- **Efficient Traffic Flow:** Firewalls manage traffic to ensure the network runs efficiently without bottlenecks.
- **Remote Access:** They enable secure remote access to a network via Virtual Private Networks (VPNs), essential for modern business environments.

Using a firewall effectively ensures that digital assets are guarded against a wide array of cyber threats. However, they must be properly configured and regularly updated to defend against evolving threats. Combining a firewall with other security measures like antivirus software and intrusion detection systems provides a comprehensive defense strategy that significantly enhances network security. This multi-layered approach is essential for maintaining the integrity and confidentiality of critical data in an increasingly connected world.

6.4 Configuring Firewall Settings

The firewall configuration process dictates how the firewall behaves in various scenarios and handles different types of network traffic. It involves specifying which service ports and IP addresses are allowed or blocked under different conditions. Effective firewall configuration strikes a balance between security and functionality, ensuring that security measures don't impede necessary network operations.

Key Aspects of Firewall Configuration:

1. **Setting Up Firewall Rules:** Firewall rules direct how the firewall should handle incoming and outgoing traffic based on factors like IP addresses, domain names, protocols, ports, and content types. Rules should follow the principle of least privilege, allowing only necessary traffic.
2. **Creating Secure Zones:** Segregate the network into secure zones to control traffic flow between different areas. This segmentation minimizes potential damage in case of a security breach.
3. **Implementing Default Deny:** Use a default deny policy to only permit traffic explicitly allowed within the firewall rules. This approach is safer than default allow policies.
4. **Regular Updates and Maintenance:** Update the firewall's firmware regularly to protect against the latest vulnerabilities and threats. Review and update firewall rules periodically to adapt to new requirements and threats.
5. **Logging and Monitoring:** Enable logging to keep records of detected and blocked threats, as well as normal and abnormal traffic patterns. Monitoring these logs helps in identifying potential security incidents early and fine-tuning firewall settings.

6. **Testing Firewall Configurations:** Regularly test firewall configurations to ensure they effectively block unauthorized access while allowing legitimate traffic. Testing helps identify misconfigurations and areas where the firewall may be too restrictive or too lenient.

Best Practices for Firewall Configuration:

- **Simplicity in Rule Definition:** Keep firewall rules simple and specific to avoid complexity, which can lead to errors and security loopholes.

- **Continuous Review and Revision:** Regularly review firewall configurations to ensure they remain effective against new threats and aligned with organizational changes.

- **Use of Role-Based Access Controls (RBAC):** Implement RBAC to manage who can configure the firewall and what changes they can make, reducing the risk of unauthorized changes.

- **Incorporating with Additional Security Systems:** Fuse the firewall with other security mechanisms such as intrusion detection systems (IDS) and security information and event management (SIEM) systems to achieve thorough protection coverage.

6.5 Best Practices for Using Antivirus and Firewalls

Best Practices for Antivirus Software:

1. **Regular Updates:** Ensure automatic updates are enabled to keep antivirus software equipped with the latest virus definitions and software updates.

2. **Comprehensive Scanning:** Schedule regular full system scans and perform manual scans on new devices or files to detect and remove any malware.

3. **Minimize Exclusions:** Limit file or application exclusions from antivirus scans to prevent potential loopholes for malware.

4. **Heuristic Settings:** Enable heuristic analysis to detect unknown viruses or malware based on behavior and adjust sensitivity settings accordingly.

5. **Integration with Other Security Tools:** Ensure antivirus software integrates well with other security tools for enhanced overall protection.

Best Practices for Firewalls:

1. **Rule Management:** Regularly review and update firewall rules to align with current network configurations and security policies, removing obsolete or unnecessary rules.

2. **Default Deny Policy:** Implement a default deny policy to block all traffic except explicitly allowed, minimizing the chances of malicious traffic slipping through.

3. **Segment Networks:** Use firewalls to create network segments, limiting the spread of attacks within the network by controlling traffic between segments.

4. **Monitor and Log Traffic:** Monitor network traffic and maintain logs, reviewing them regularly to detect unusual activity indicating a security breach.

5. **Regular Testing:** Periodically test firewall configurations to ensure they effectively block unauthorized access while allowing legitimate traffic, identifying weaknesses for improvement.

Combined Strategies for Antivirus and Firewalls:

1. **Layered Security Approach:** Use antivirus software and firewalls together as part of a layered security strategy for comprehensive protection against cyber threats.

2. **Consistent Updates and Reviews:** Regularly update antivirus definitions and firewall rules, conducting reviews of security policies and configurations to adapt to new threats.

3. **User Education:** Train users on the importance of security measures, including not disabling antivirus or firewall protections and recognizing signs of malware.

4. **Regular Backups:** Maintain regular backups of important data for data integrity and recovery in case of a malware attack.

Conclusion:

Effectively using antivirus software and firewalls involves continuous management, regular updates, strategic rule setting, vigilant monitoring, and integration within a broader security framework. By following these best practices, individuals and organizations can significantly strengthen their defenses against the ever-evolving landscape of cyber threats.

Chapter 7: Cybersecurity at Work

7.1 Security Protocols for the Workplace

Developing a Comprehensive Security Framework

1. **Access Control:** Utilize sophisticated systems like role-based access control (RBAC) to meticulously manage permissions, ensuring employees only access necessary resources.

2. **Data Encryption:** Protect sensitive data stored on company servers and during its transfer over the internet by encrypting it, ensuring it remains inaccessible to unauthorized users.

3. **Network Security:** Strengthen defenses against vulnerabilities by implementing firewalls, intrusion detection systems, and secure Wi-Fi protocols, while consistently updating and patching network devices.

4. **Authentication Protocols:** Enhance user authentication processes with strong, unique passwords and multi-factor authentication (MFA) for robust identity verification.

5. **Regular Audits and Monitoring:** Conduct security audits and continuously monitor network and system activities to detect suspicious behavior and potential threats early for prompt responses.

6. **Physical Security:** Implement measures to prevent unauthorized physical access to company facilities, including security personnel, surveillance systems, and secured entry points.

7. **Incident Response Plan:** Develop an agile incident response plan outlining procedures for containment, investigation, eradication, recovery, and post-incident analysis in the event of a security breach.

8. **Vendor Risk Management:** Assess and control interactions with external vendors accessing the organization's data or systems, imposing stringent security requirements and conducting regular evaluations.

Integrating Security Into Corporate Culture

1. **Employee Training:** Provide continual training programs educating employees about cybersecurity, covering topics like recognizing phishing scams, handling sensitive information, and adhering to safe internet practices.

2. **Policy Updates and Communication:** Evolve security policies to reflect dynamic cyber threats and organizational changes, communicating updates promptly and clearly to ensure all staff understand their roles and responsibilities.

3. **Technology Use Policies:** Establish clear policies for technology use, including guidelines on mobile devices, remote work, and personal device usage at work to prevent security breaches from poor technology practices.

Implementing robust security protocols and fostering a security-conscious culture is essential for safeguarding organizational data, reputation, and operational integrity. By meticulously planning, implementing, and updating security measures, organizations can protect themselves against a wide array of digital threats, ensuring their continued success in the ever-evolving landscape of cybersecurity.

7.2 Handling Sensitive Data

Sensitive data encompasses information requiring protection due to its confidentiality, such as personal identifiers, financial details, health information, and intellectual property. It can exist in various formats, from digital files on a network to physical documents.

Strategies for Effective Data Handling

1. **Data Classification:** Identify and classify sensitive data based on its level of sensitivity and potential risk. This guides how data should be handled and protected.

2. **Access Controls:** Implement robust access control measures to restrict access to sensitive data to authorized personnel only, using encryption and authentication mechanisms.

3. **Data Encryption:** Encrypt sensitive data at rest and in transit to convert it into a format that cannot be easily understood without the correct decryption key.

4. **Regular Audits and Monitoring:** Continuously monitor how sensitive data is accessed and used, conducting regular audits to assess policy adherence and identify areas for improvement.

5. **Secure Data Storage and Transmission:** Utilize secure storage solutions and encrypted communication channels to maintain the integrity and confidentiality of sensitive data.

6. **Data Minimization and Retention:** Collect only necessary data and implement strict retention policies to minimize stored data. Dispose of data securely when no longer needed.

7. **Training and Awareness:** Educate employees about data security, their roles in handling sensitive data, potential risks, and the organization's data privacy policies.

Integrating Data Protection into Business Operations

1. **Policy Development:** Create clear policies for handling sensitive data, outlining procedures and responsibilities that align with industry standards and compliance requirements.

2. **Incident Response:** Develop an incident response plan for potential data breaches, including steps for containment, investigation, notification, and remediation.

3. **Vendor Management:** Ensure third-party vendors handling sensitive data comply with security standards, incorporating security requirements into contracts and conducting regular audits.

7.3 Compliance Requirements: GDPR, HIPAA

GDPR (General Data Protection Regulation):

- Enforced by the European Union (EU) to protect the personal data and privacy of its citizens.
- Applies to all companies operating within the EU and those outside the EU offering goods or services to EU data subjects.
- Key requirements include explicit consent for data processing, individuals' rights to access and control their data, data protection measures, and reporting data breaches within specified timeframes.

HIPAA (Health Insurance Portability and Accountability Act):

- A US law providing privacy standards for patients' medical records and other health information.
- Developed by the Department of Health and Human Services, it sets standards for privacy, security, and breach notification.
- Key provisions include the Privacy Rule (protecting medical records), Security Rule (securing electronic protected health information), and Breach Notification Rule (requiring notification following a breach).

Strategies for Compliance

1. **Data Protection Officer (DPO):**
   - Designate a Data Protection Officer (DPO) to supervise data security strategy and compliance, guaranteeing adherence to GDPR policies and procedures.

2. **Risk Evaluations:**
   - Regularly perform risk assessments to pinpoint vulnerabilities in data handling and storage, prioritize security enhancements, and showcase compliance.

3. **Education and Consciousness:**
   - Educate staff about GDPR and HIPAA obligations through regular training, ensuring they understand the importance of compliance and know how to handle sensitive information.

4. **Policies and Procedures:**
   - Formulate and execute robust policies and procedures consistent with GDPR and HIPAA standards, encompassing data collection, storage, transfer, and deletion.

5. **Breach Notification Protocols:**
   - Establish protocols for detecting, reporting, and investigating personal data breaches, ensuring timely internal reporting and compliance with reporting requirements to authorities and affected individuals.

6. **Vendor Compliance:**
   - Ensure third-party vendors handling personal or health information comply with GDPR and HIPAA by carefully selecting vendors and including compliance obligations in vendor contracts.

Navigating the complexities of GDPR and HIPAA is challenging but essential for organizations handling personal or health-related information. By implementing rigorous data protection measures, conducting regular compliance checks, and fostering a culture of data privacy and security, organizations can comply with regulations and build trust with customers and clients.

7.4 Security Training for Employees

Importance of Regular and Engaging Training

Effective security training engages employees and imparts essential knowledge regularly to maintain awareness and readiness. Frequent sessions reflect the latest cybersecurity trends and threats, incorporating interactivity like quizzes, workshops, and simulations to reinforce learning and practical application.

Tailoring Content to the Audience

Customizing training content to fit each department's unique risks ensures relevance and practicality. IT staff may need technical training on network defenses, while customer service teams benefit from learning about social engineering and phishing defense strategies.

Communication and Policy Integration

Training should communicate the organization's security policies and expectations, clarifying roles and responsibilities regarding data protection, IT resource usage, sensitive information handling, and incident reporting.

Building a Culture of Security

The goal is to foster a culture of security characterized by vigilance, informed caution, and proactive behavior. Regular assessments and updates to the training program ensure relevance and adaptability to new challenges.

Implementation Strategies

1. **Baseline Assessment:** Determine the current level of security knowledge to tailor training effectively.
2. **Scheduled Training:** Establish a regular schedule for sessions, remaining flexible to incorporate updates when new threats emerge.
3. **Feedback Mechanisms:** Encourage participant feedback to refine and improve sessions continuously.
4. **Accountability:** Integrate security training into job performance evaluations to emphasize its importance and ensure active participation.

7.5 Dealing with Security Breaches

Understanding Security Breaches

Security breaches involve unauthorized access to data, networks, or devices, potentially leading to theft, corruption, or disruption. They vary in scope and impact, affecting personal data to critical operational systems.

Preparation: The Key to Effective Response

1. **Incident Response Plan:** Comprehensive plan outlining procedures, roles, responsibilities, and communication strategies, regularly updated to reflect new threats and changes.

2. **Regular Drills and Training:** Simulate breaches to ensure the incident response team can act quickly and effectively. Provide training for all employees to recognize signs and take appropriate actions.

Responding to a Security Breach

1. **Detection and Identification:** Quick detection is crucial; employ monitoring tools for real-time detection of unusual activity.

2. **Containment:** Immediately contain the breach to minimize disruption. Disconnect infected parts of the network, revoke access permissions, or take systems offline as necessary.

3. **Eradication and Recovery:** Remove the root cause, patch vulnerabilities, and restore systems and data from clean backups.

4. **Notification and Communication:** Comply with legal requirements, notify affected individuals and regulatory bodies promptly, and communicate transparently with stakeholders.

5. **Post-Incident Analysis:** Conduct a thorough analysis to identify weaknesses, assess the response, and make necessary improvements to security strategies.

Building Resilience

1. **Learning from Breaches:** Use insights gained from post-incident analyses to enhance incident response plans and overall security strategies.

2. **Investing in Security:** Regular investments in updated technologies, training, and security measures are crucial to keep pace with evolving threats.

Chapter 8: Social Engineering and Human Factors

8.1 Understanding Social Engineering Attacks

Social Engineering Attacks Overview

Social engineering attacks leverage psychological manipulation instead of traditional hacking methods to access buildings, systems, or data. These attacks typically involve tricking people into violating standard security protocols. It's crucial to understand the mechanics and underlying principles of these attacks to effectively counter them.

Essence of Social Engineering

At its core, social engineering exploits basic human instincts—like the tendency to help others, avoid conflicts, or trust in authority. Attackers manipulate these traits to coax individuals into revealing confidential information, allowing unauthorized access, or undertaking actions that jeopardize security. The reliance on human mistakes makes these attacks particularly perilous, as human error is often the most vulnerable aspect of security systems.

Prevalent Social Engineering Strategies

1. **Pretexting:** Attackers concoct believable scenarios to earn trust. For example, they might impersonate colleagues, law enforcement, bank employees, or other authorities to gather personal information.

2. **Phishing:** This tactic involves sending deceptive emails or messages from seemingly credible sources to trick recipients into disclosing sensitive data or clicking links that deploy malware.

3. **Baiting:** Similar to phishing, baiting offers enticing items in return for private information. An example is leaving a USB stick marked "Confidential" in a visible area, which installs malware when used.

4. **Tailgating:** Here, an intruder gains access to a restricted space by following someone with legitimate access.

5. **Quid pro quo:** Attackers offer a fake benefit in exchange for information, such as a hacker posing as tech support asking for login credentials to solve a nonexistent problem.

Why Social Engineering is Effective

Social engineering thrives by exploiting natural human behaviors that are advantageous in harmless situations, like being accommodating or trusting. Attackers are adept at reading these behaviors and exploiting the willingness to help. Moreover, the complexities of the digital realm and the burden of maintaining numerous passwords can induce security fatigue, which attackers exploit by proposing simple fixes or aid.

Consequences of Social Engineering

The effects of successful social engineering attacks are severe, including substantial financial losses, unauthorized data access, data breaches, and eroded customer trust. The indirect costs, like reputational damage and increased security spending after an attack, can also be significant.

8.2 Examples of Social Engineering Attacks

Overview of Social Engineering Attacks

Social engineering attacks exploit various human vulnerabilities, and understanding these through real-world examples helps organizations strengthen their defenses. This section highlights key techniques used by attackers to manipulate individuals and infiltrate organizational security.

Phishing: The IRS Scam

A frequent phishing scheme involves impostors claiming to be from the Internal Revenue Service (IRS) to extract personal data. Victims receive emails seemingly from the IRS about an urgent matter needing immediate resolution. These emails usually contain links leading to bogus websites where victims are prompted to input their sensitive information.

Baiting: The USB Drop Technique

This form of baiting involves leaving a malware-laden USB drive in areas like company parking lots or lobbies. Unsuspecting employees may find these drives and plug them into their computers out of curiosity, inadvertently installing malware. This method exploits human curiosity and the appeal of seemingly free items.

Pretexting: Impersonating IT Support

In pretexting scenarios, the fraudster crafts a situation to gather personal details from their target. Here, the perpetrator might pretend to be an IT support agent contacting employees under the guise of performing routine checks or addressing an issue, requesting login credentials or remote computer access. Employees often comply, mistakenly believing they are aiding a legitimate company operation.

Tailgating: Gaining Unauthorized Access

Tailgating involves an unauthorized person stealthily following someone with proper clearance into a restricted area. This might occur when an attacker walks closely behind a person with access or asks someone to hold a door open, exploiting social norms and the individual's reluctance to deny such a request.

Quid Pro Quo: Offering Free Tech Support

In this tactic, the attacker poses as a tech support worker offering free security checks or technical assistance, contacting random employees within a company. During the interaction, they might solicit login credentials or persuade the employee to install remote desktop software, purportedly for maintenance, thereby gaining uncontrolled access.

Strategies for Understanding and Prevention

These incidents emphasize the need for continuous vigilance and skepticism towards unexpected communications and offers that seem overly advantageous. To safeguard against social engineering threats, organizations should:

- Continually educate their workforce about social engineering risks and their various forms.
- Enforce security policies that instruct employees on managing unsolicited requests for sensitive data.
- Promote the use of multifactor authentication and strong, unique passwords to minimize unauthorized access risks.
- Ensure a secure physical environment to deter unauthorized facility access.

8.3 Training Employees to Recognize Social Engineering Attacks

Training programs that equip employees to detect and counter social engineering are essential elements of an organization's cybersecurity framework. Since these attacks exploit psychological rather than technical vulnerabilities, awareness and targeted education are fundamental in defending against these tactics. This segment outlines effective strategies for educating employees on recognizing and thwarting social engineering efforts.

Building an Effective Training Initiative

Effective training against social engineering requires continuous learning and reinforcement, not just a one-off session. Key strategies to develop a robust training program include:

- **Ongoing Training**: Hold regular sessions to keep security top of mind for employees. Update these sessions often to include the latest tactics used by social engineers and to share relevant real-world incidents.

- **Simulated Experiences**: Use simulations of social engineering scenarios, such as phishing emails or pretexting calls, to give employees practical experience. This hands-on approach helps embed the lessons learned, enhancing their ability to respond to actual threats.

- **Diverse Learning Materials**: Employ a variety of educational materials to suit different learning preferences. This might include videos, interactive quizzes, and group workshops, all designed to engage and involve participants actively.

- **Behavioral Focus**: Aim to change behaviors, not just impart knowledge. Highlight the personal and organizational consequences of security breaches to stress the importance of vigilant behavior.

- **Real Incident Analysis**: Include case studies of recent social engineering attacks, particularly those relevant to the organization or its industry. Analyzing these incidents helps make the training relatable and underscores the importance of vigilance.

Essential Training Focus Areas

- **Phishing Recognition**: Educate employees on spotting suspicious emails and links. Teach them to look for signs like spelling errors, generic salutations, and urgent requests that pressure immediate action.

- **Managing Unsolicited Information Requests**: Train employees on handling unexpected information requests via email, phone, or in person, emphasizing the importance of verifying identities through independent methods.

- **Secure Communication Practices**: Ensure all employees are aware of the correct procedures for sharing sensitive information and the steps for verifying requests.

- **Understanding Manipulative Tactics**: Explain the psychological techniques commonly employed by social engineers, such as exploiting authority or creating a sense of urgency, so employees can recognize when they're potentially being manipulated.

Reinforcing Training Insights

- **Continuous Improvement**: Maintain ongoing security education with regular updates on new threats and refreshers on security practices to keep awareness sharp.

- **Supportive Reporting Environment**: Foster a workplace culture where employees feel safe to report unusual activities without fear of negative consequences. Establish clear, straightforward reporting procedures.
- **Incentives and Rewards**: Implement incentives or gamification to boost engagement and participation in security training. Rewards for teams excelling in security drills, for instance, can motivate all employees to take training seriously.

8.4 Building a Security Culture at Work

Creating a strong security culture is vital for defending against cyber threats, including social engineering. Such a culture integrates security awareness and behaviors into the daily activities of every employee across all organizational levels. This section outlines effective strategies to cultivate a security-focused environment where safeguarding information is a universal priority.

Foundations of a Strong Security Culture

Building a resilient security culture hinges on fostering awareness, responsibility, and proactive practices across the entire organization, not just within IT departments.

- **Leadership Involvement:** It's crucial that organizational leaders champion security initiatives. They should actively engage in security practices and training, setting a strong example for all team members to emulate.
- **Education and Training:** Ongoing education is crucial to maintain and enhance security awareness. Training should be frequent, captivating, and customized to address the unique risks each department faces. This keeps employees informed about the latest threats and defensive tactics.
- **Clear Policies and Protocols:** Developing and sustaining transparent, accessible security policies is essential. These guidelines should clearly outline expected behaviors and the procedures to follow under various circumstances. Regular updates to these policies keep them relevant.

Strategies for Enhancing Security Culture

- **Empowerment Through Knowledge:** Providing employees with the knowledge to make informed security decisions in their daily tasks is essential. They should understand the implications of their actions and know how to recognize and address security threats effectively.
- **Open Communication:** Create an atmosphere where security discussions, questions, and incident reporting are encouraged without fear of negative repercussions. Open lines of communication enable employees to share insights that may help identify weaknesses and refine existing protocols.
- **Simulation Exercises:** Regularly scheduled drills and simulations that replicate potential real-life security breaches can offer employees practical experience. These simulations ensure that the training remains relevant and engaging.
- **Recognition and Incentives:** Encouraging secure behavior through recognition and rewards can significantly enhance commitment to security protocols. Whether through awards, public acknowledgment, or bonuses, incentivizing security-minded actions can reinforce their importance.

- **Integration into Company Culture:** Embedding security into the company's core values is achievable by regularly including security topics in meetings, newsletters, and corporate events. This helps to underline security's role in the organization's overall success.

Measuring Security Culture Effectiveness

- **Regular Assessments:** Periodic evaluations are necessary to gauge the strength and efficacy of the security culture. Techniques like surveys, interviews, and analysis of security incidents play a crucial role in these assessments.
- **Feedback Loops:** Establishing feedback mechanisms is key to learning from both security failures and successes. These loops not only aid in the continuous enhancement of security measures but also keep the dialogue around security active.

8.5 Personal Vigilance: Protecting Yourself and Others

In cybersecurity, personal vigilance is a crucial complement to technical security measures, involving individual awareness and proactive actions to recognize and counteract potential security threats.

Understanding Personal Vigilance

Personal vigilance is the ongoing attentiveness and cautious behavior required to protect sensitive information and computing resources. It involves being conscious of potential security risks in daily activities and making deliberate efforts to avoid or reduce these risks.

Key Components of Personal Vigilance

- **Awareness of Security Practices**: It's vital to stay updated on best security practices and organizational policies, including understanding the dynamics of cyber threats like phishing, malware, and social engineering.

- **Regular Updates and Maintenance**: Keep all personal and organizational devices updated with the latest security patches and software enhancements. Outdated systems are vulnerable to attacks that exploit known weaknesses.

- **Secure Password Practices**: Employ strong, distinct passwords for various accounts and enable multi-factor authentication when possible. Using a reputable password manager can help manage different passwords securely.

- **Physical Security Measures**: Maintain physical security by locking devices with passwords or biometric safeguards and avoiding leaving them unattended in public spaces. Make sure sensitive information is not exposed to onlookers on your screens.

Practices to Enhance Personal Vigilance

- **Continuous Learning**: The cybersecurity landscape is constantly changing, making it crucial to stay informed. Regular participation in training sessions, webinars, and courses helps keep up-to-date with security trends and practices.

- **Use of Security Tools**: Employ security tools like antivirus software, firewalls, and encrypted backups. These tools add a layer of protection and assist in detecting and addressing threats.

- **Reporting Suspicious Activities**: Actively report any suspicious activities or security incidents to the relevant department within your organization. Prompt reporting can drastically minimize the damage from a security breach.

- **Secure Communication**: Always use secure communication channels when handling sensitive information. Be mindful about sharing any sensitive personal or organizational data over unsecured platforms.

- **Personal Device Management**: Handle your personal devices with care, particularly those used for work. Ensure these devices comply with organizational security standards and are protected as rigorously as office equipment.

Chapter 9: Introduction to Risk Management

9.1 Basics of Cybersecurity Risk Assessment

Cybersecurity risk assessment is an essential process that enables organizations to identify, evaluate, and prioritize risks to their information assets. This critical step in risk management examines potential threats to both digital and physical infrastructures and assesses the likelihood and impact of these threats materializing. Grasping the fundamentals of cybersecurity risk assessment is crucial for devising strategies to mitigate these risks effectively.

What is Cybersecurity Risk Assessment? A cybersecurity risk assessment is a systematic evaluation aimed at identifying vulnerabilities within an organization's information systems and the risks these vulnerabilities pose. It analyzes potential threats to the organization's assets and the vulnerabilities that could be exploited by these threats, causing damage to the organization.

Key Components of Cybersecurity Risk Assessment

- **Asset Identification**: The process begins with identifying and classifying assets that require protection, including data, software, hardware, infrastructure, intellectual property, and personal data of employees and customers.

- **Threat Identification**: Following asset identification, potential threats to these assets are listed, ranging from natural disasters and system failures to cyber threats like phishing, malware, and ransomware.

- **Vulnerability Assessment**: This step involves pinpointing weaknesses in the organization's current security measures that could be exploited by identified threats. Common vulnerabilities include outdated software, weak passwords, or inadequate security policies.

- **Impact Analysis**: Assess the potential impact of a breach or security incident for each asset-threat combination. This evaluation helps in prioritizing risks based on their potential severity.

- **Likelihood Determination**: Estimate the probability of each risk occurring, taking into account factors such as the external threat environment, effectiveness of existing controls, and historical security incident data.

The Process of Conducting a Risk Assessment

- **Establish the Context**: Begin by understanding the organization's environment, objectives, and the policies and processes that will frame the risk assessment.

- **Risk Analysis**: Analyze the identified risks to evaluate their impact and likelihood. This can be done using qualitative measures or quantitative measures.

- **Risk Evaluation**: Assess the analyzed risks against the organization's predefined risk criteria to determine which risks require mitigation, helping prioritize actions based on the organization's risk tolerance.

- **Documentation**: Thoroughly document the risk assessment process, including details of identified risks, their analysis, and evaluation. This documentation is vital for future risk treatment and provides an audit trail for decisions made.

Importance of Regular Risk Assessments Cybersecurity risk assessments should be a continuous activity within an organization's risk management practices. Regular assessments are crucial to adapt to changes in the external threat landscape and internal operations, which can alter the organization's risk profile.

9.2 Tools and Techniques for Risk Management

Effective risk management in cybersecurity combines various tools and techniques to help organizations identify, assess, and mitigate risks. This systematic approach ensures consistency, repeatability, and scalability in managing security risks across the organization. This subchapter delves into the essential tools and techniques that significantly contribute to effective cybersecurity risk management.

Risk Management Tools

- **Automated Risk Assessment Tools**: These tools automate the process of identifying vulnerabilities and assessing risks by scanning networks and systems. They evaluate potential impacts and prioritize risks based on set criteria. Examples include Nessus, Qualys, and Rapid7.

- **GRC Platforms**: Governance, Risk Management, and Compliance (GRC) platforms provide an integrated approach to managing governance, risk, and compliance issues. These platforms help organizations consolidate and manage risk management practices across departments. Well-known GRC tools include RSA Archer, IBM OpenPages, and ServiceNow GRC.

- **SIEM Systems**: Security Information and Event Management (SIEM) systems offer real-time analysis of security alerts from applications and network hardware. They are essential for detecting, analyzing, and responding to security incidents, providing timely insights that are crucial for risk management. Popular SIEM tools are Splunk, LogRhythm, and AlienVault.

- **Threat Intelligence Platforms**: These platforms deliver information on emerging or current threats and threat actors, enabling organizations to proactively adjust their risk management strategies. Examples include FireEye, Recorded Future, and CrowdStrike.

Risk Management Techniques

- **Risk Identification Workshops**: These workshops engage stakeholders from various departments to identify potential risks, fostering a comprehensive understanding of risks and their sources across the organization.

- **SWOT Analysis**: Employing a Strengths, Weaknesses, Opportunities, and Threats (SWOT) analysis helps identify internal and external factors affecting risk. This technique is valuable for understanding the organization's cybersecurity strengths and vulnerabilities.

- **Root Cause Analysis**: Following a risk event, root cause analysis determines the underlying causes of the risk, which is crucial for developing strategies to prevent future similar risks.

- **Scenario Analysis**: This technique involves creating potential risk event scenarios and modeling their possible outcomes to understand the impacts of different risk events better and guide the development of effective risk mitigation strategies.

Integrating Tools and Techniques

Integrating these tools and techniques into a cohesive risk management strategy ensures they complement each other, providing a comprehensive approach to risk management. For example, while automated tools can perform routine risk assessments, workshops and SWOT analysis offer deeper insights into strategic risk management challenges.

9.3 Identifying and Mitigating Risks

Effective risk management in cybersecurity is crucial for accurately identifying potential risks and implementing strategies to mitigate them. This critical phase allows organizations to prioritize resources and apply targeted security measures to safeguard their information and systems. The following outlines the process for identifying and mitigating risks within a cybersecurity framework.

Identifying Risks

Risk identification is a thorough analysis of the organization's environment to pinpoint factors that could lead to a security incident. This involves several key steps:

- **Asset Inventory**: Start by cataloging all assets, categorizing them based on importance and sensitivity. This includes physical devices, information assets, software applications, and services.

- **Threat Assessment**: Evaluate the threats each asset may face, including external threats like cybercriminals, malware, and phishing, as well as internal threats such as employee errors and insider attacks.

- **Vulnerability Evaluation**: Identify vulnerabilities that could be exploited by these threats. This may involve software vulnerabilities, inadequacies in security policies, or physical security weaknesses.

- **Existing Controls Review**: Assess the effectiveness of existing security controls in mitigating identified vulnerabilities to determine if enhancements are needed.

Mitigating Risks

Once risks are identified, the focus shifts to managing these risks through mitigation strategies, which includes:

- **Risk Prioritization**: Assess risks according to their potential impact and likelihood of occurrence, enabling efficient resource allocation towards addressing the most significant threats.

- **Risk Treatment Options**: Choose the best approach for managing each risk, which could include:
  - **Risk Sharing**: Transferring the risk to another entity, such as through insurance.
  - **Risk Avoidance**: Changing plans to sidestep the risk.
  - **Risk Reduction**: Introducing controls to lessen the impact or likelihood of the risk.
  - **Risk Acceptance**: Accepting the risk when mitigation costs outweigh potential benefits.

- **Control Implementation:** Deploy targeted security measures and controls to mitigate risks. This may entail technical solutions like firewalls, encryption, and intrusion detection systems, alongside administrative controls such as training and policy updates.
- **Continuous Monitoring and Review**: Consistently monitor the effectiveness of the controls and adjust as necessary. This ongoing review ensures that mitigation strategies are effective and remain responsive to evolving threats.

Documenting the Risk Management Process

- **Risk Register**: Keep a risk register that logs all identified risks, their assessments, and the actions taken to mitigate them. This register is a dynamic document that outlines the risk landscape and organizational responses.
- **Reporting and Communication:** Consistently update senior management and other stakeholders on risk management advancements. Effective communication is essential for fostering a collective comprehension of the risk landscape and the importance of implemented controls.

9.4 Continual Risk Evaluation

Continual risk evaluation is a critical component of an organization's risk management strategy, ensuring that cybersecurity defenses are effectively tailored and responsive to the dynamic nature of threats. This ongoing process enables organizations to adjust to changes in their operational environment, embrace emerging technologies, and respond to evolving threat landscapes.

The Importance of Continual Risk Evaluation

Cybersecurity is an ever-changing field, with new threats emerging as attackers refine their techniques and capitalize on new vulnerabilities. Additionally, changes within the organization—such as the introduction of new technologies, adjustments in business processes, or organizational restructuring—can shift the risk landscape. Continual risk evaluation ensures that an organization's risk management strategies stay aligned with its current threat environment and business goals.

Key Elements of Continual Risk Evaluation

- **Regular Assessments**: These are crucial for revisiting and evaluating existing security measures and the overall risk landscape. It involves re-assessing previously identified risks to see if their likelihood or impact has changed.
- **Monitoring for New Threats and Vulnerabilities**: Keeping abreast of the latest security threats and vulnerabilities that could affect the organization is essential. This can be achieved through threat intelligence feeds, participation in security forums, and the deployment of automated monitoring tools.
- **Integrating Feedback Mechanisms**: Effective risk management incorporates feedback from security incidents, audits, and employee observations. This continuous input is vital for pinpointing areas needing enhancement in cybersecurity practices.

- **Revising Risk Mitigation Strategies**: Continual risk evaluations might necessitate updates or modifications to existing security controls, the introduction of new technologies, or changes in operational procedures to tackle new or changing risks.
- **Training and Awareness Programs**: Keep training programs updated to reflect new cybersecurity trends and threats, ensuring all employees understand their role in safeguarding the organization and are prepared to manage emerging threats.

Techniques for Effective Continual Risk Evaluation

- **Automated Monitoring Tools**: Employ advanced monitoring tools for real-time insights into the organization's networks and systems. These tools help detect anomalies that might indicate new security threats or vulnerabilities.
- **Risk Dashboards**: Create risk dashboards that visually represent the organization's risk status. These dashboards track key metrics and changes over time, aiding in quick decision-making and reporting.
- **Scenario Analysis and Stress Testing**: Conduct regular scenario analysis and stress testing to assess the organization's resilience against specific cyberattacks or its capability to handle the failure of certain systems, identifying potential weaknesses.
- **Engaging External Experts**: Engage external cybersecurity experts periodically to perform independent assessments of the organization's security measures. External reviews offer a fresh perspective and can uncover areas of improvement that might be overlooked by internal teams.

9.5 Creating a Risk Management Plan

Creating a comprehensive risk management plan is crucial for any organization looking to effectively shield itself from cybersecurity threats. This plan acts as a blueprint, guiding the organization through the steps of identifying, assessing, managing, and mitigating risks in a structured and deliberate way. This subchapter outlines the essential steps needed to develop a robust risk management plan that aligns with an organization's unique needs and security requirements.

Steps to Develop a Risk Management Plan

1. **Establish the Context**: Start by defining the scope and objectives of the risk management plan, ensuring alignment with the organization's strategic goals. Consider both internal and external factors that influence the risk environment. Understanding the context is crucial for tailoring risk management processes to the organization's specific operations.

2. **Risk Identification**: Identify the risks that could potentially impact the organization systematically. This includes cyber threats like malware, ransomware, phishing, data breaches, and risks arising from internal processes or external factors. Techniques such as brainstorming, interviews, and technical assessments can facilitate thorough risk identification.

3. **Risk Analysis**: Evaluate the identified risks to assess their potential impact and likelihood. This analysis will aid in understanding the extent of risks and their possible effects on the organization. Employ both qualitative and quantitative methods to determine the severity of each risk.

4. **Risk Evaluation**: Prioritize the risks based on their analysis. This step helps determine which risks are acceptable and which necessitate immediate action or mitigation strategies. Prioritizing risks ensures that resources are allocated efficiently, concentrating efforts on managing higher-priority risks.

5. **Risk Mitigation Strategies**: Develop plans to handle or mitigate identified risks. These could involve avoiding risks altogether, implementing controls to minimize their impact, sharing the risk through insurance or partnerships, or accepting risks that fall within the organization's tolerance levels. The chosen strategy should consider the risk's priority and the organization's ability to effectively manage it.

6. **Implementation**: Execute the risk mitigation strategies. This involves allocating resources, setting timelines, and delegating responsibilities to team members. Effective implementation typically requires extensive communication and collaboration across various departments.

7. **Monitoring and Review**: Continuously monitor the risk environment and the effectiveness of the strategies implemented. Conduct regular reviews to evaluate the necessity for adjustments in response to operational changes or shifts in the external environment. This step is essential for ensuring the continued relevance and effectiveness of the risk management plan.

8. **Communication and Reporting**: Maintain clear communication with all stakeholders regarding the status of risk management activities. Regular reporting promotes transparency and aids senior management in making informed decisions. Effective communication also encompasses training and educating staff about their roles in the risk management process.

Integrating the Risk Management Plan into Corporate Culture

For a risk management plan to be effective, it must be ingrained in the organization's day-to-day activities and corporate culture. Promoting a risk-aware culture involves ongoing dialogue about risks, integrating risk management into decision-making processes, and incentivizing risk-conscious behaviors.

Chapter 10: Preparing for Cyber Incidents

10.1 Steps to Prepare for a Cyber Incident

Preparing for a cyber incident is a critical aspect of an organization's cybersecurity strategy, involving proactive planning to effectively respond to cyber threats and minimize damage.

Establishing a Cybersecurity Framework

- **Risk Assessment**: Begin by conducting a comprehensive risk assessment to identify potential cybersecurity threats This helps prioritize areas where defenses need to be strengthened.
- **Asset Identification**: Catalog all critical assets, including data, hardware, software, and systems, to determine what needs protection and to implement appropriate security measures.

Developing Incident Response Capabilities

- **Incident Response Team Formation**: Gather a multidisciplinary team comprising members from departments like IT, legal, public relations, and human resources to spearhead response endeavors during a cyber incident.
- **Communication Channels**: Establish clear internal and external communication channels. Internally, this ensures swift communication among team members during an incident. Externally, it facilitates necessary communications with stakeholders, customers, or regulatory bodies.
- **Legal and Regulatory Compliance:** Grasp and adhere to legal and regulatory obligations concerning cybersecurity in your jurisdiction, including mandates for reporting breaches and cooperating with authorities.

Implementing Preventative

- **Measures**: • Security Measures: Deploy strong security measures derived from risk assessment results, such as firewalls, antivirus software, encryption, and intrusion detection systems.
- **Data Backup**: Routinely back up crucial data and ensure backups are securely stored and readily retrievable to address data loss incidents.
- **Access Controls**: Enforce stringent access controls and authentication protocols to limit access to sensitive information and vital systems.

Training and Awareness

- **Employee Training**: Regularly train all employees on cybersecurity best practices and specific procedures to follow during a cyber incident to reduce the risk of human error-caused incidents.
- **Simulation Exercises**: Routinely simulate cyber incidents to test the organization's preparedness, evaluate the effectiveness of the incident response plan, and train the incident response team and staff in their roles during an actual incident.

10.2 Creating an Incident Response Plan

Crafting a proficient Incident Response Plan (IRP) is vital for organizations to effectively handle and alleviate cyber incidents. This plan acts as a detailed roadmap, guiding the response team through essential steps needed to handle security breaches or attacks effectively.

Key Elements of an Incident Response Plan

- **Preparation**: This foundational step involves establishing the necessary tools, policies, and procedures to address incidents. At the core of this stage is establishing an incident response team with well-defined roles and responsibilities.

- **Identification**: Establish protocols for promptly detecting incidents. This involves monitoring systems and networks for indications of security breaches and having predefined procedures for responding to identified anomalies.

- **Containment**: After identifying an incident, the immediate focus should shift to containment to prevent further damage. This involves implementing short-term strategies to stop the immediate threat and long-term solutions to ensure the threat is fully eradicated and unlikely to recur.

- **Eradication**: This step involves addressing the root cause of the incident, which may include removing malware, disabling compromised accounts, or updating vulnerable software to prevent future breaches.

- **Recovery:** Reestablish and normalize operations of affected systems while meticulously verifying their integrity and ensuring they are devoid of vulnerabilities and malware. This phase typically involves comprehensive validation of system integrity and ongoing monitoring for potential vulnerabilities.

- **Lessons Learned**: Post-incident, conduct a thorough review to evaluate the response's effectiveness and identify areas for improvement. Insights gained should be integrated back into the IRP to enhance future responses.

Steps to Create an Incident Response Plan

- **Define and Classify Incidents**: Clearly define what constitutes a security incident and categorize incidents based on their severity to facilitate prioritized responses and resource allocation.

- **Develop Communication Guidelines**: Establish protocols for managing communications during an incident, delineating internal communication among team members and external communication with stakeholders, media, and regulators.

- **Delegate Roles and Responsibilities**: Clarify and allocate roles and responsibilities within the incident response team. Each member should understand their designated tasks and contribution to the overall response endeavor.

- **Develop Response Procedures for Different Scenarios**: Craft tailored response procedures for various cyber incident types, such as ransomware attacks, data breaches, or DDoS attacks. Customized procedures help ensure that responses are both efficient and effective.

- **Integrate with Business Continuity Plans**: Align the incident response plan with the organization's broader business continuity planning to ensure coherent recovery processes and minimal operational disruption.

- **Regular Testing and Drills**: Periodically test the IRP through drills and simulations to identify any gaps and ensure team readiness for actual incidents.
- **Continuous Review and Improvement**: Given the dynamic nature of cyber threats, regularly review and update the IRP to include new threats, technological advancements, and changes in business operations.

10.3 The Importance of Regular Plan Updates

In the dynamic realm of cybersecurity, threats evolve rapidly, necessitating that incident response plans (IRPs) be regularly updated to remain effective. A plan that isn't frequently updated may quickly become outdated, leaving an organization vulnerable to new cyber threats. Regular revisions of the IRP are crucial to ensure that it remains effective and that the organization is well-prepared for any security incident.

Reasons for Regular Updates

- **Evolving Threat Landscape**: Cyber threats continually evolve as attackers develop new methods and exploit fresh vulnerabilities. Regular updates to the IRP ensure that it keeps pace with the latest security challenges.
- **Technological Advancements**: As organizations adopt new technologies, their cyber risk profiles change. Updates to the IRP can reflect changes such as the adoption of cloud computing, the integration of IoT devices, or updates in software and hardware systems.
- **Organizational Changes**: Shifts in business operations like mergers, acquisitions, or expansions into new markets introduce new risks. These changes, along with adjustments in personnel or structure, may affect roles and responsibilities within the response team, requiring updates to the IRP.
- **Lessons Learned from Incidents**: Each cyber incident offers valuable insights that can enhance future responses. Incorporating lessons learned from past incidents and drills into the IRP is essential for improving its effectiveness.
- **Regulatory and Legal Changes**: As laws and regulations evolve, compliance requirements may change. Regular updates to the IRP help ensure ongoing compliance with all applicable legal and regulatory frameworks.

Steps to Ensure Effective Updates

- **Scheduled Reviews**: Implement a regular schedule for reviewing and updating the IRP. The frequency of these reviews should align with the organization's exposure to risk and its rate of operational change, whether annually, semi-annually, or quarterly.
- **Incorporate Stakeholder Feedback**: Engage a diverse group of stakeholders in the review process, including representatives from IT, security teams, legal, HR, and public relations. This inclusive approach helps ensure that the plan comprehensively addresses all aspects of the organization's operations.

- **Test and Revise**: Regularly conduct drills and simulations to test the IRP's effectiveness. Analyze the outcomes of these exercises to pinpoint weaknesses and areas for improvement, using these insights to refine the plan.

- **Stay Informed**: Keep up-to-date with the latest trends in cybersecurity and threat intelligence. This ongoing awareness can inform necessary adjustments to the IRP, strengthening its defenses against emerging threats.

- **Document Changes**: Keep meticulous records of all changes made to the IRP. Documentation should include reasons for the changes, aiding in future audits and reviews and providing a historical context for the evolution of the response strategy.

10.4 Simulation and Training

Simulation and training are essential elements of a robust cybersecurity strategy, particularly in preparing for and responding to cyber incidents. Regular simulation of cyber attacks and training exercises are crucial to ensure that both the incident response team and all employees are prepared to act swiftly and effectively under pressure.

Importance of Simulation and Training

- **Enhanced Preparedness**: Simulations offer a realistic experience of potential cyber incidents, helping teams understand and internalize the necessary procedures for actual events, thereby boosting their overall readiness.

- **Skill Development**: Regular training and simulation exercises are vital for developing and refining the skills needed to identify, respond to, and mitigate cyber threats. These activities ensure that the team remains sharp and familiar with the latest tactics employed by cyber attackers.

- **Response Efficacy**: Routine testing of the incident response plan through simulations allows organizations to assess the effectiveness of their response strategies. This evaluation helps pinpoint weaknesses and areas where enhancements are needed.

- **Improved Communication**: Simulations improve communication and coordination within the incident response team and across the organization. Efficient communication is critical during a real cyber incident to ensure a successful response.

Strategies for Effective Simulation and Training

- **Regular Drills**: Conduct regular drills to simulate a variety of cyber incidents, such as phishing, malware attacks, data breaches, and system outages. These drills should include not only IT and security teams but also other departments like communications, legal, and executive management.

- **Scenario-Based Training**: Create training modules based on realistic scenarios that could impact the organization. These should reflect the specific cyber threats relevant to the organization's risk profile and industry.

- **Use of Advanced Tools**: Utilize advanced simulation tools that can emulate a broad range of cyber threats in a controlled setting. Cyber range platforms, for example, offer a highly realistic simulation environment beneficial for training purposes.

- **Cross-Departmental Exercises**: Engage various departments in the simulations to ensure that all parts of the organization understand their roles during a cyber incident. This inclusive approach helps ensure that incident response transcends the technical response and incorporates the entire organizational structure.

- **Feedback and Evaluation**: After each simulation or training session, conduct a thorough debrief to identify what was successful and what areas need improvement. This feedback should inform adjustments to the incident response plan and enhance the quality of future training exercises.

- **Continuous Learning**: Continually update training and simulation programs to incorporate new information, tactics, and insights gleaned from recent cyber incidents—both internal and external. Keeping the training content current is crucial for maintaining its relevance and effectiveness.

10.5 Responding to a Cyber Incident

When a cyber incident occurs, the speed and effectiveness of the response can critically influence the severity and scope of damage to an organization. A well-coordinated response can minimize both immediate and long-term consequences.

Immediate Steps in Responding to a Cyber Incident

1. **Detection and Identification**: Prompt and accurate identification of the cyber incident is crucial. This requires ongoing monitoring and advanced detection systems that can alert the organization to potential breaches.

2. **Containment**: Once an incident is identified, the next step is containment to prevent further damage. This may involve isolating affected systems, restricting network access, or temporarily shutting down certain operations to halt the spread of the attack.

3. **Eradication**: After containment, focus shifts to eliminating the threat from the environment. This includes deleting malicious files, disabling breached accounts, and patching vulnerabilities exploited during the attack.

4. **Recovery**: Begin recovery by restoring affected systems and data from clean backups. Thoroughly check all restored systems for any signs of the attacker's presence before reconnecting them to the network.

5. **Communication**: Maintain clear and timely communication with all stakeholders throughout the response process, including internal management, employees, customers, partners, and if necessary, the public. Effective communication is essential to manage the situation and maintain trust.

Deeper Strategic Response Considerations

- **Forensic Analysis**: Conduct a thorough forensic investigation to understand how the breach occurred, which data or systems were affected, and whether any data was stolen or tampered with. This analysis is crucial for preventing future incidents and may be necessary for legal and compliance purposes.

- **Legal and Regulatory Compliance**: Review the incident with respect to legal and regulatory requirements to determine if the breach must be reported to authorities or affected individuals. Compliance is crucial to avoid legal penalties.

- **Review and Update Incident Response Plan**: After managing the incident, review the effectiveness of the incident response plan and the organization's actual response. Update the plan based on lessons learned and any new threats identified during the forensic analysis.

- **Ongoing Monitoring and Vigilance**: Post-incident, maintain heightened monitoring to detect any signs that the attacker may attempt to regain access. It's common for attackers to leave backdoors that can be used to re-enter the network.

Training and Preparedness

- **Regular Training**: Ensure that all relevant personnel are trained and familiar with the incident response plan. Frequent practice exercises and simulations can aid in readying the team for actual incidents.

- **Updating Skills and Tools**: Continually enhance the skills of the cybersecurity team and update the tools they use to respond to incidents. Staying ahead of evolving cyber threats requires ongoing education and investment in technology.

Chapter 11: Emerging Technologies and Future Threats

11.1 Summary of Up-and-Coming Cybersecurity Technologies

As cyber threats become more sophisticated, the field of cybersecurity is constantly evolving, introducing new and emerging technologies aimed at strengthening defense mechanisms and enhancing security protocols.

Advanced Threat Detection Systems

- **Machine Learning and AI-powered Security**: With the integration of machine learning and artificial intelligence, security systems can anticipate, identify, and counter threats more swiftly and precisely compared to conventional approaches. These systems leverage historical data to identify patterns and deviations suggestive of potential security risks.

- **Behavioral Analytics**: This technology analyzes the behaviors of users, entities, and networks to identify deviations from normal activities that could signal a security incident. It is especially useful for detecting insider threats and compromised accounts.

Enhanced Defensive Mechanisms

- **Automated Security Orchestration and Response (SOAR)**: SOAR platforms enhance the efficiency of security operations centers (SOCs) by integrating various security tools and automating responses to cyber threats. This automation of routine tasks allows security professionals to concentrate on addressing more sophisticated threats.

- **Next-Generation Firewalls (NGFW)**: NGFWs extend beyond traditional packet filtering and port/protocol inspection by incorporating advanced features such as application-level inspection, intrusion prevention, and external intelligence integration.

Proactive Threat Management

- **Deception Technology**: This strategy employs decoys and traps within the network that mimic legitimate systems to deceive attackers. This allows organizations to detect and analyze attack methods safely without risking actual data or systems.

- **Zero Trust Models**: Operating under the principle of "never trust, always verify," zero trust models represent a departure from traditional network security that assumed trust for devices within a security perimeter. This model enforces strict identity verification for anyone and any device attempting to access network resources, regardless of their location relative to the network perimeter.

Privacy Enhancements

- **Homomorphic Encryption**: An innovative encryption method that allows data to be encrypted and processed in its encrypted form, thus maintaining data privacy and security simultaneously. This method enables the analysis or processing of encrypted data without decryption, safeguarding the data even from the entities performing the computations.

- **Secure Access Service Edge (SASE):** SASE represents a leading-edge cybersecurity concept that integrates network security functionalities with WAN capabilities to address organizations' evolving secure access requirements. It amalgamates solutions such as SD-WAN, firewall-as-a-service, and zero-trust network access into a consolidated service model.

11.2 Predictions on Future Cyber Threats

Increased Sophistication of Attacks

- **AI-Powered Attacks**: With artificial intelligence (AI) becoming more sophisticated, the potential for its malicious use increases. Future cyber threats may involve AI-driven attacks that can learn and adapt in real-time, making them tougher to detect and neutralize. For instance, AI might be utilized to craft highly personalized and effective phishing emails.

- **Advanced Ransomware Tactics**: Ransomware attacks are expected to not only become more frequent but also more sophisticated, targeting critical infrastructure and employing advanced techniques to evade detection and enhance impact. Future ransomware could dynamically adjust its ransom demands based on the encrypted data's sensitivity and the victim's financial capabilities.

Expansion of Attack Surfaces

- **Internet of Things (IoT) Vulnerabilities**: As IoT devices proliferate across personal, public, and corporate spaces, they are likely to introduce new vulnerabilities. Numerous IoT devices lack robust security features, rendering them vulnerable targets for cybercriminals aiming to infiltrate larger networks.

- **5G and Network Security**: The deployment of 5G technology will enhance internet speed and connection reliability but also bring new security challenges. The enhanced speed and connectivity could allow attackers to initiate and propagate attacks more swiftly than before.

Emerging Areas of Concern

- **Deepfakes and Information Integrity**: The advancement of deepfake technology poses significant threats in misinformation and fraud. With easier access to more convincing tools, these could be used to produce fraudulent media that damages personal reputations or influences public opinion and elections.

- **Supply Chain Attacks**: Cyber threats may increasingly target supply chains, exploiting vulnerabilities in less secure network elements. These attacks can have extensive effects, impacting multiple organizations simultaneously and disrupting operational and logistical systems.

Responding to Future Cyber Threats

- **Proactive Defense Strategies**: Organizations must adopt proactive cybersecurity measures, such as advanced predictive analytics tools, to identify and neutralize potential threats before they materialize.

- **Regulatory and Legal Frameworks**: As cyber threats evolve, governments worldwide may introduce stricter regulatory frameworks to protect consumers and businesses. Organizations will need to stay informed and adapt quickly to comply with new regulations.

- **Education and Training**: Consistent education and training for both cybersecurity experts and general staff are imperative. Staying updated on emerging threats and comprehending how to avert and address attacks are vital for upholding security.

11.3 Preparing for AI and Machine Learning in Cybersecurity

Artificial Intelligence (AI) and Machine Learning (ML) are revolutionizing cybersecurity, introducing new defense mechanisms and challenges. As these technologies become essential components of cybersecurity strategies, it's vital for organizations to effectively integrate them while recognizing potential risks and vulnerabilities.

Understanding AI and ML in Cybersecurity

AI and ML are capable of rapidly analyzing extensive data sets to detect patterns indicative of threats, far surpassing human analytical capabilities. These technologies adapt and evolve in response to changing attack tactics, making them invaluable for dynamic threat detection, behavioral analysis, and automated responses.

Strategic Implementation of AI and ML

- **Invest in Talent and Training**: Equip your workforce to manage AI and ML technologies by investing in specialized training for your IT and cybersecurity teams. Understanding these technologies' strengths and limitations is crucial.

- **Choose the Right Tools**: Evaluate AI and ML cybersecurity products to find those that best meet your organization's specific needs, infrastructure, and risk profile.

- **Data Management**: AI and ML require high-quality data to be effective. Ensure your organization can securely collect, store, and process large datasets, maintaining data integrity and confidentiality.

Integrating AI and ML into Existing Systems

- **Gradual Integration**: Initiate small-scale pilot projects to assess the effectiveness of AI and ML in your environment, allowing for adjustment and scalability without jeopardizing your entire security framework.

- **Continuous Monitoring**: Constant monitoring and oversight are crucial, as AI and ML systems may err, especially when confronted with sophisticated or novel attacks. Human oversight ensures errors are identified and addressed promptly.

- **Update and Maintenance**: Regularly update and maintain AI models to ensure they stay effective as cyber threats evolve.

Addressing Potential Risks

- **Security of AI Systems**: Protect AI and ML systems from cyberattacks, including both external threats and insider risks.

- **Bias and Reliability**: AI systems may exhibit biases from their training data, potentially impacting decision-making. Continuously fine-tune training datasets and algorithms to minimize bias and improve reliability.

- **Dependency and Complacency**: While AI and ML are powerful, avoid over-reliance on these technologies. They should enhance, not replace, traditional cybersecurity methods and human judgment.

Preparing for the Future

- **Stay Updated**: Stay abreast of the latest advancements in AI and ML to comprehend how developments might impact your cybersecurity strategy.
- **Ethical Considerations**: Consider the ethical implications of using AI and ML, particularly regarding privacy and data use. Adherence to ethical guidelines and best practices is essential for maintaining trust and compliance.

11.4 The Role of Blockchain in Security

Blockchain technology, primarily known for its application in cryptocurrencies like Bitcoin, presents considerable potential for bolstering cybersecurity across various industries. Its core characteristics—decentralization, transparency, and immutability—make it an advantageous tool for securing data and transactions against increasing cyber threats.

Understanding Blockchain's Core Features

- **Decentralization**: Unlike traditional databases that centralize data storage, blockchain distributes data across a network of computers. This decentralization helps mitigate the risks linked to single points of failure, which are common vulnerabilities in centralized systems.
- **Transparency**: Blockchain ensures that all transactions are visible to every network participant and can be audited in real-time. This level of transparency is critical in building trust among users and is particularly valuable in applications requiring data integrity and comprehensive audit trails.
- **Immutability**: Transactions documented on a blockchain remain unalterable and irreversible. This permanence secures data integrity and makes blockchain a formidable tool against data manipulation and fraud.

Applications of Blockchain in Cybersecurity

- **Secure Data Storage**: Blockchain offers a robust platform for creating tamper-proof data records. For industries like healthcare, finance, and legal, which demand high data integrity, blockchain provides a secure means to store sensitive information.
- **Identity Verification**: Blockchain can significantly enhance identity verification processes, making it extremely difficult for unauthorized users to fabricate identities. Utilizing blockchain to manage digital identities helps streamline authentication processes while safeguarding personal data.
- **IoT Security**: As the number of IoT devices escalates, securing these devices and their data transfers becomes increasingly challenging. Blockchain can facilitate secure, autonomous interactions between IoT devices by establishing a decentralized network that supports secure and resilient data exchanges.

- **Decentralized DNS**: Cyberattacks, such as DDoS, often exploit the centralized nature of the Domain Name System (DNS). Decentralizing DNS entries across multiple nodes via blockchain significantly increases the difficulty for cybercriminals to hijack URLs and redirect traffic to malicious sites.

Challenges in Implementing Blockchain for Security

- **Scalability**: Blockchain technology currently faces scalability issues, as many blockchain architectures can only process a limited number of transactions per second, potentially insufficient for large-scale applications.

- **Complexity and Cost**: Deploying blockchain technology demands substantial expertise and investment. The technology's complexity also poses integration challenges with existing IT systems.

- **Regulatory and Legal Issues**: Being a relatively new technology, blockchain encounters various regulatory challenges. The absence of definitive regulatory guidelines poses significant hurdles for organizations, especially those in highly regulated sectors.

Preparing for Blockchain Integration

- **Education and Training:** Companies should allocate resources to education and training programs to cultivate in-house blockchain proficiency.

- **Pilot Projects**: Initiating small-scale pilot projects can allow organizations to gauge blockchain's benefits and challenges before committing extensive resources to broader implementations.

- **Collaboration and Standardization**: Collaborating with other entities and industry groups to develop standards and best practices for using blockchain in cybersecurity can help overcome challenges related to scalability and interoperability.

Blockchain technology holds promising potential to enhance cybersecurity through its intrinsic properties of decentralization, transparency, and immutability. However, harnessing this potential effectively requires addressing significant challenges related to scalability, complexity, and regulatory compliance. By carefully evaluating their specific needs and the readiness of blockchain solutions, organizations can strategically incorporate this technology to strengthen their cybersecurity defenses.

Chapter 12: Continuing Your Cybersecurity Education

12.1 Resources for Further Learning

In the dynamic world of cybersecurity, ongoing education is essential to keep pace with rapidly evolving technologies, tactics, and trends. This subchapter highlights a variety of resources available to professionals aiming to expand their knowledge and stay at the forefront of the cybersecurity field. These resources include online platforms, professional publications, conferences, workshops, and more.

Online Learning Platforms

- **Coursera and edX**: Coursera and edX offer a broad selection of cybersecurity courses taught by university professors or industry experts, spanning from beginner to advanced levels.

- **Udemy and Pluralsight**: Renowned for practical, skills-based learning, these platforms provide courses tailored to both novices and seasoned professionals. Topics include ethical hacking, penetration testing, and cybersecurity for cloud computing.

- **Cybrary**: Dedicated specifically to cybersecurity, Cybrary offers a mix of free and premium resources that cover various domains such as CISSP, CompTIA Security+, and ethical hacking.

Professional Publications and Journals

- **The SANS Reading Room**: Features research papers and articles written by seasoned cybersecurity professionals, covering a wide array of topics from current issues to foundational principles.

- **Security Magazine**: Delivers articles, webinars, and case studies on the latest trends in security management, risk assessment, and crisis management, serving as a valuable resource for all professional levels.

- **IEEE Security & Privacy**: This bimonthly magazine provides peer-reviewed articles on the latest industry trends and developments, catering to those who prefer a scholarly approach to cybersecurity education.

Conferences and Workshops

- **Black Hat and DEF CON**: Attending these conferences can offer deep insights into the latest cybersecurity research, vulnerabilities, and defensive techniques, presented by leading security experts globally.

- **RSA Conference**: Features a range of sessions from technical presentations to discussions on policy and strategy, offering a prime networking opportunity and a chance to learn from industry thought leaders.

- **Local Workshops and Meetups**: Engaging in local events not only aids in acquiring new skills but also in building a network with other cybersecurity professionals within your region.

Government and Institutional Resources

- **NIST Cybersecurity Framework**: Provides comprehensive standards, guidelines, and best practices for managing cybersecurity-related risks. The NIST website is a valuable tool for implementing effective cybersecurity strategies at the organizational level.
- **Cybersecurity & Infrastructure Security Agency (CISA)**: Offers training, publications, and alerts on cybersecurity threats and vulnerabilities, crucial for professionals seeking to enhance their expertise and stay informed on national security trends.

Peer Groups and Forums

- **Online Forums like Reddit's r/cybersecurity**: Engaging with peers on platforms like Reddit or specialized forums such as Stack Exchange is an excellent way to exchange knowledge, discuss new developments, and address specific queries.
- **LinkedIn Groups**: By joining cybersecurity-related groups on LinkedIn, professionals can keep up with industry updates and share best practices and insights with peers globally.

12.2 Cybersecurity Courses and Certifications

Cybersecurity courses and certifications are essential for professionals looking to validate their skills and advance their careers. These educational tools not only enhance knowledge and expertise but also provide credentials that are highly respected in the industry.

Foundational Courses and Certifications

- **CompTIA Security+**: This certification serves as an excellent starting point for anyone seeking to acquire a broad understanding of security concepts, tools, and procedures. It covers crucial principles for network security and risk management, establishing a foundational knowledge base for a cybersecurity career.
- **Cisco Certified CyberOps Associate**: This certification focuses on security operations, equipping professionals for roles in security analysis and network administration. It provides essential skills needed to effectively respond to cybersecurity incidents as part of a security team.

Advanced Certifications

- **Certified Information Systems Security Professional (CISSP)**: Administered by (ISC)², the CISSP is a distinguished certification designed for seasoned security professionals, managers, and leaders. It validates proficiency across various security practices and principles.
- **Certified Information Security Manager (CISM)**: Provided by ISACA, this certification is geared towards those who manage, design, oversee, and assess an organization's information security. It focuses on governance and management, making it ideal for leadership roles.
- **Certified Ethical Hacker (CEH)**: This certification, from EC-Council, trains professionals to understand and use hacking techniques legally to conduct penetration testing. It aims to teach professionals to think like hackers to better defend against future attacks.

Specialized Courses and Certifications

- **Offensive Security Certified Professional (OSCP)**: This hands-on certification is revered in the cybersecurity community. It tests a candidate's ability to identify vulnerabilities and conduct controlled attacks, demonstrating a practical understanding of offensive security.
- **NIST Cybersecurity Framework (NCSF)**: Focused on the framework devised by the National Institute of Standards and Technology, this certification aids professionals in comprehending and executing current standards for adeptly managing cybersecurity risks.

Vendor-Specific Certifications

- **AWS Certified Security - Specialty**: Tailored for IT security experts engaged with Amazon Web Services, this certification attests to an individual's proficiency in safeguarding AWS data and workloads.
- **Microsoft Certified: Azure Security Engineer Associate**: This certification focuses on securing data, applications, and networks in Microsoft Azure and hybrid environments. It demonstrates expertise in implementing security controls and maintaining a secure posture.

Importance of Continuous Education

Cybersecurity is a constantly evolving field; thus, continuous education through courses and certifications is vital to stay updated with the latest security technologies, practices, and regulations. Acquiring certifications not only boosts professional credibility and career prospects but also ensures that cybersecurity professionals' skills and knowledge remain current and relevant.

12.3 Building a Career in Cybersecurity

Cybersecurity is a dynamic and rapidly expanding sector within the tech industry, driven by the growing complexity and frequency of cyber threats. For those looking to build or advance a career in cybersecurity, a combination of education, skill development, and strategic career planning is essential.

Educational Foundations

- **Formal Education**: Though not always required, a degree in computer science, information technology, cybersecurity, or a related field can provide a solid theoretical base and a competitive advantage in the job market. Many universities now offer specialized courses dedicated to cybersecurity.
- **Certifications**: Earning industry-recognized certifications such as CompTIA Security+, CISSP, or CISM can significantly bolster your credentials and demonstrate your commitment and expertise to prospective employers.

Gaining Practical Experience

- **Internships and Entry-Level Positions**: Gain practical experience through internships or entry-level roles such as security analyst, network administrator, or IT technician. These positions offer firsthand exposure to the cybersecurity challenges that organizations encounter daily.
- **Hands-On Training**: Engage in hands-on training sessions, workshops, and cyber competitions like CTFs (Capture The Flag). These experiences cultivate practical skills and problem-solving abilities essential for a career in cybersecurity.

Specialization Areas

- **Choose a Specialization**: Cybersecurity encompasses various specializations, including penetration testing, malware analysis, network security, and cybersecurity policy. Focusing on a specific area can make you an expert and enhance your marketability.
- **Continuous Learning**: The cybersecurity landscape is continually evolving. Keep abreast of the latest threats and technologies by following industry news, attending conferences, webinars, and pursuing ongoing education and training.

Networking and Professional Development

- **Professional Networks**: Join professional organizations such as ISACA, (ISC)², and regional cybersecurity groups. Networking with peers can provide insights into industry trends, career advice, and job opportunities.
- **Mentorship**: Pursue mentorship from seasoned professionals who can provide guidance, career counsel, and constructive feedback. Mentors offer valuable insights and assist in navigating your career path successfully.

Soft Skills Development

- **Communication Skills**: Effective written and verbal communication skills are crucial. Cybersecurity professionals often need to explain complex technical issues to non-technical stakeholders.
- **Problem-Solving Skills**: The ability to think critically and solve complex problems swiftly is vital in a field where threats can arise suddenly and escalate quickly.
- **Ethical Integrity**: Cybersecurity professionals handle sensitive information and must uphold the highest levels of integrity and ethical standards.

By adopting these strategies, individuals can effectively prepare for a successful career in cybersecurity, ensuring they are well-equipped to handle the challenges and opportunities in this evolving field.

12.4 Staying Current: The Importance of Continuous Learning

The necessity for continuous learning in cybersecurity is crucial due to the fast-paced evolution of threats, technologies, and regulatory requirements.

Evolving Threat Landscape: Cybercriminals continually refine their tactics and techniques. Keeping abreast of the latest threats is essential for effectively safeguarding systems and data.

Technological Advancements: As technologies like artificial intelligence, machine learning, and blockchain become increasingly prevalent in cybersecurity, professionals must learn to effectively implement and manage these tools.

Regulatory Changes: Cybersecurity is subject to stringent regulations that can vary by industry and region. Professionals must stay informed on these changes to ensure compliance.

Strategies for Continuous Learning

- **Formal Education and Training**: Enroll in courses and workshops to refresh and expand your skill set. Many educational institutions and organizations offer specialized training in areas such as cloud security, ethical hacking, and data privacy.
- **Certifications**: Pursuing certifications is a dual benefit—enhancing your professional credentials while necessitating ongoing education to maintain these certifications. This structured learning ensures professionals continuously update their skills.
- **Professional Communities**: Join organizations like ISACA, (ISC)², or local cybersecurity groups. These associations offer access to resources such as journals, professional development programs, and community forums.
- **Online Resources**: Utilize online platforms including blogs, podcasts, and newsletters focused on cybersecurity. These are valuable for quick insights into current trends and practices.
- **Research and Publications**: Engaging with current research through peer-reviewed journals and industry reports is crucial. Contributing articles or papers on cybersecurity topics can also deepen your knowledge and establish you as a thought leader.

Benefits of Continuous Learning

- **Enhanced Skills and Knowledge**: Staying current through continuous learning enables professionals to effectively counteract new and evolving threats.
- **Career Advancement**: Continuous learning equips professionals with the latest knowledge and skills, preparing them for advancement into higher-level roles that demand a current and comprehensive skill set.
- **Networking Opportunities**: Educational events like courses and seminars are excellent venues for networking. These connections can be instrumental for collaborative learning and career advancement.
- **Resilience Against Job Market Changes**: The cybersecurity job market is dynamic, with frequent shifts in needed skills and technologies. Those committed to continuous learning are well-prepared to adapt and capitalize on new opportunities as they emerge.

12.5 Networking and Professional Development in Cybersecurity

Networking and professional development are pivotal elements in forging a successful career in cybersecurity. Engaging with peers, mentors, and industry leaders provides valuable avenues for learning, collaboration, and career advancement.

Importance of Networking in Cybersecurity

- **Knowledge Sharing**: Cybersecurity evolves rapidly. Networking enables professionals to exchange knowledge, share best practices, and stay abreast of the latest threats and technologies, maintaining a cutting-edge understanding of the field.
- **Career Opportunities**: Many cybersecurity positions are filled through networking rather than public job postings. Networking can lead to job offers, collaborative projects, and freelance opportunities, often initiated through personal recommendations or connections.

- **Support and Mentorship**: Relationships with experienced professionals provide mentorship, guidance, and support. These connections are invaluable for navigating the complexities and challenges of a cybersecurity career.

Strategies for Effective Networking

- **Professional Associations**: Joining organizations like ISACA, (ISC)², or local cybersecurity groups is an excellent way to meet peers. These groups often organize conferences, workshops, and training sessions that facilitate networking.

- **Conferences and Seminars**: Participating in industry events such as Black Hat, DEF CON, or the RSA Conference is perfect for engaging with a diverse group of professionals, learning from experts, and discussing industry trends.

- **Online Communities**: Engaging in online forums, social media groups, and platforms like LinkedIn allows networking beyond geographical constraints, which is particularly useful for connecting with international colleagues.

- **Local Meetups and Hackathons**: Attending local gatherings and cybersecurity competitions offers hands-on experience and networking in a less formal environment, fostering community ties.

Professional Development in Cybersecurity

- **Continuous Education**: Continual learning through certifications, courses, and webinars is essential to maintain relevant skills and knowledge in a fast-evolving field.

- **Certification Programs**: Advanced certifications like CISSP, CISM, and CEH not only deepen expertise but also enhance professional stature. These credentials are globally recognized and can significantly boost career prospects.

- **Public Speaking and Presentation**: Developing public speaking skills through presentations at conferences and seminars can establish a professional as a thought leader within the cybersecurity community.

- **Mentoring Others**: Offering mentorship to newcomers not only hones leadership skills but also provides fresh insights into personal practices and strategies.

- **Publishing Articles and Papers**: Writing and publishing on cybersecurity topics enhances visibility and credibility and establishes influence within the field.

Chapter 13: Career Opportunities in Cybersecurity

13.1 Sector-Wise Demand for Cybersecurity Professionals

The demand for cybersecurity professionals continues to surge across diverse sectors, fueled by an increased reliance on digital technologies and a rising tide of cyber threats. As industries recognize the vital importance of protecting their data and systems, the opportunities for cybersecurity experts are expanding rapidly.

Financial Services

The financial sector, including banks, investment firms, and insurance companies, consistently ranks as a prime target for cyberattacks due to the highly sensitive financial data it manages. There is a robust demand for cybersecurity professionals skilled in safeguarding transactions, protecting customer data, and ensuring compliance with stringent financial regulations such as GDPR, PCI DSS, and Sarbanes-Oxley.

Healthcare

The healthcare industry faces significant cybersecurity challenges, intensified by the digitization of medical records and the expanding use of IoT devices. Professionals here are essential for defending patient data against breaches, securing connected medical devices, and adhering to rigorous standards like HIPAA in the United States.

Government and Defense

Government and national security agencies demand stringent cybersecurity to protect sensitive data and critical infrastructure. In this sector, professionals are tasked with countering national security threats, securing communication systems, and safeguarding data pertinent to national defense and other governmental operations.

Technology and Software

Technology companies, from burgeoning startups to major players like Google, Microsoft, and Amazon, constantly require cybersecurity experts. These professionals are crucial for protecting intellectual property, securing cloud services, preventing data breaches, and developing secure software solutions.

Retail and E-commerce

As retail entities expand their online operations, their vulnerability to cyber threats like payment fraud and data breaches increases. Cybersecurity experts in this sector focus on securing online transactions, safeguarding customer data, and ensuring the security of e-commerce activities.

Energy and Utilities

The energy sector, including utilities managing water, gas, and electricity, faces potential cyberattacks that could disrupt essential services. Cybersecurity professionals in this field are responsible for protecting critical infrastructure, complying with industry-specific regulations, and securing operational technology.

Education

Educational institutions increasingly recognize the necessity of cybersecurity to protect student data, research materials, and digital learning platforms. In this sector, cybersecurity roles often involve enhancing network security, improving data privacy, and ensuring the safety of digital learning environments.

Telecommunications

With advancements in network technologies such as 5G, telecommunications companies are prioritizing cybersecurity to protect infrastructure, secure data transmission, and maintain service integrity against disruptions from cyber threats.

Automotive

The automotive industry faces novel cybersecurity challenges as vehicles become more connected and autonomous. Professionals in this field work on securing connected car technologies, protecting vehicle communication systems, and ensuring passenger safety from cyber-physical threats.

13.2 Emerging Roles in Cybersecurity

As technological advancements continue and cyber threat dynamics evolve, the cybersecurity landscape is witnessing the emergence of new roles requiring specialized skills and knowledge.

Cybersecurity Analyst

A Cybersecurity Analyst oversees the monitoring of an organization's networks and systems to detect security breaches, conducts investigations into incidents, and implements requisite security measures. This role involves conducting vulnerability testing, risk analyses, security assessments, and developing organizational security procedures like disaster recovery plans and incident response protocols.

Threat Hunter

Threat Hunters proactively search through networks to detect and isolate advanced threats that elude existing security measures. This role demands a profound understanding of the organization's IT environment and an attacker's mindset, utilizing data analytics and threat intelligence to hypothesize potential threats, identify security lapses, and suggest improvements.

Chief Information Security Officer (CISO)

Increasingly strategic, the role of the CISO involves aligning security initiatives with business objectives and overseeing IT security department operations. CISOs play a crucial role in communicating with the board and other executives to keep them informed about security risks and solutions.

Security Architect

Security Architects are responsible for designing, constructing, testing, and deploying security systems within an organization's IT infrastructure. They develop intricate security frameworks to ensure they proficiently deter breaches and thwart hacking endeavors.

Penetration Tester

Also known as ethical hackers, Penetration Testers simulate cyber attacks to identify system vulnerabilities before they can be exploited maliciously. This role is essential as organizations increasingly depend on digital platforms and need to secure them against external and internal threats.

Incident Response Specialist

Focusing on managing security breaches, Incident Response Specialists work to restore and secure data and systems post-attack. They possess strong forensic skills and an understanding of relevant laws to effectively mitigate damage and aid in recovery.

Cloud Security Specialist

With the shift towards cloud computing, Cloud Security Specialists are vital for securing cloud-based platforms. They develop cloud-specific security policies, secure data transfers, and manage compliance challenges associated with cloud environments.

IoT Security Specialist

As IoT devices proliferate, IoT Security Specialists are crucial for addressing the unique security challenges these devices present. They focus on device security, data protection, and ensuring network security across extensive networks of connected devices.

13.3 Navigating the Cybersecurity Job Market

Navigating the cybersecurity job market can be both exciting and daunting, given the field's rapid expansion and the constant evolution of threats and technologies. Whether you're just starting your career or seeking advancement, understanding the dynamics of the cybersecurity job market is crucial for securing the right opportunities.

Understanding the Market Demand

- **Broad Scope of Opportunities**: Cybersecurity professionals are in demand across various sectors such as government, finance, healthcare, retail, and technology. Each sector presents unique security challenges and a range of roles, creating diverse career paths.

- **Geographic Trends**: Some regions offer more opportunities than others due to industry concentration. Tech hubs like Silicon Valley and urban centers like New York City and Washington, D.C., are hotspots for cybersecurity talent due to the prevalence of tech companies and government agencies.

Skills and Qualifications

- **Technical Proficiency**: It's vital to stay current with the latest technologies, security protocols, and countermeasure techniques. Skills in network security, encryption, and ethical hacking are particularly valued.

- **Certifications**: Earning certifications such as CISSP, CISM, CompTIA Security+, or CEH can significantly boost your job prospects by validating your expertise and knowledge.

- **Soft Skills**: Effective communication of complex security concepts to non-technical stakeholders is essential. Additionally, problem-solving, critical thinking, and strong interpersonal skills are crucial in cybersecurity roles.

Job Search Strategies

- **Leverage Professional Networks**: Networking is a powerful tool in the cybersecurity job market. Engage with professional groups, online forums, and local meetups to connect with peers and industry leaders who might provide job leads and advice.
- **Utilize Job Boards and Recruitment Agencies**: Many companies post openings on general job boards, but specific platforms for tech and cybersecurity jobs can also be useful. Recruitment agencies specializing in cybersecurity can help tailor your job search to your skills and career aspirations.

Preparing for Interviews

- **Research Potential Employers**: Understand the specific security challenges of the industry and the employer. Tailor your approach to demonstrate how your skills and experiences align with their needs.
- **Showcase Problem-Solving Skills:** Be ready to discuss your approach to security challenges, perhaps with examples of how you've successfully managed security issues in the past.
- **Stay Informed About Industry Trends**: Demonstrating knowledge of recent cybersecurity incidents or emerging threats can showcase your dedication and passion for the field.

Career Development

- **Continuous Learning:** Cybersecurity is an ever-evolving field; staying informed about new technologies, threats, and mitigation strategies is essential for maintaining a competitive edge.
- **Seek Mentoring and Guidance**: Having a mentor experienced in cybersecurity can provide invaluable career advice, help in skill development, and expand your professional network.

13.4 Long-Term Career Development in Cybersecurity

Building a long-term career in cybersecurity goes beyond technical acumen; it demands continuous learning, adaptability, and strategic career planning. As the cybersecurity landscape evolves with new threats and technologies, professionals must actively manage their career trajectories to remain relevant and effective.

Setting Career Goals

- **Define Your Career Objectives**: Set clear, specific career goals to guide your professional development and decisions. Whether aiming to become a Chief Information Security Officer (CISO), specialize in areas like penetration testing, or become a thought leader, having defined objectives is crucial.
- **Regular Self-Assessment**: Periodically evaluate your skills, certifications, and professional experiences. Identify any gaps or areas needing improvement and align these with your career goals to strategically plan your next steps.

Continuous Education and Certification

- **Stay Educated**: The realm of cybersecurity is in a constant state of evolution. To stay current with the latest developments and acquire new skills, it's essential to participate in ongoing education through courses, workshops, webinars, and conferences.

- **Pursue Advanced Certifications**: Consider obtaining advanced certifications that align with your career goals as you progress. Certifications like CISSP, CISA, or those specializing in areas such as cloud security, ethical hacking, or forensics can significantly enhance your professional standing and open new career opportunities.

Gaining Diverse Experience

- **Seek Varied Roles**: Broaden your experience by taking on different roles and projects within your organization or externally. Experiences in risk assessment, incident response, compliance, and policy development are invaluable.

- **Cross-Functional Skills**: Develop competencies outside of traditional cybersecurity tasks, such as project management, leadership, and strategic planning. These skills are crucial as you transition to higher management roles or lead significant projects.

Networking and Professional Engagement

- **Build a Professional Network**: Continuously cultivate and expand your professional network. Engage in industry events, forums, and join professional organizations. Networking can unlock new collaboration opportunities, mentoring, and potential job prospects.

- **Mentorship and Peer Support**: Seek mentorship from seasoned professionals and consider mentoring others. This reciprocal relationship can enhance your leadership skills and contribute positively to the cybersecurity community.

Leadership and Specialization

- **Specialize in a Niche**: As your career advances, specializing in a niche area of cybersecurity that piques your interest can position you as an expert, making you highly sought-after in fields like IoT security, AI in cybersecurity, or cybersecurity law.

- **Develop Leadership Capabilities**: If you aspire to senior management or executive roles, focus on cultivating leadership abilities. Learn to manage teams effectively, communicate with stakeholders clearly, and make strategic decisions.

Personal Branding

- **Establish a Personal Brand**: Build your personal brand as a cybersecurity professional by sharing insights through blogs, speaking engagements, or social media. Increasing your visibility and credibility in the field can lead to more opportunities and reinforce your professional reputation.

Made in the USA
Middletown, DE
30 January 2025